"I've always made a total effort,
even when the odds
seemed entirely against me.
I never quit trying..."

ARNOLD PALMER

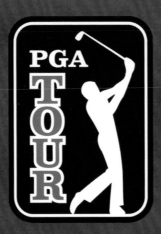

# These Guys are Good

CONTRIBUTORS

BOB CULLEN

MELANIE HAUSER    DAVID BARRETT

MARK SOLTAU    TOM MACKIN

FOREWORD

PHIL MICKELSON

TEHABI
*sports*

*These Guys are Good* was developed and published by Tehabi Sports, an imprint of Tehabi Books, Inc. Tehabi is the official book publishing licensee of the PGA TOUR and has produced and published many award-winning sports and other non-fiction books that are recognized for their strong literary and visual content. Tehabi works with national and international brands, corporations, institutions, and nonprofit groups to identify, develop, and implement comprehensive publishing programs. Tehabi Books is located in San Diego, California. *www.tehabi.com*

*President and Publisher:* **Chris Capen**
*Senior Vice President:* **Sam Lewis**
*Vice President and Creative Director:* **Karla Olson**
*Director, PGA Tour Publishing Program:* **Marci Weinberg**
*Director, Corporate Publishing:* **Chris Brimble**
*Manager, Corporate Sales:* **Andrew Arias**

*Senior Art Director:* **Charles McStravick**
*Designer:* **Jen Cadam**
*Production Artists:* **Monika Stout, Mark Santos, Helga Benz, Kendra Triftshauser**

*Editor:* **Terry Spohn**
*Editorial Assistant:* **Emily Henning**
*Contributing Writer:* **Tom Mackin: The First Tee and other PGA TOUR and player charity essays**
*Copy Editor:* **Lisa Wolff**
*Proofreader:* **Dawn Mayeda**

With special thanks to key individuals at the PGA TOUR for their invaluable contributions in the creation of *These Guys are Good:* Donna Orender, Senior Vice President, Strategic Development; Robert J. Combs, Senior Vice President, Public Relations and Communications; Ward Clayton, Director, Editorial Services; and John Snow, Director of Creative and Photographic Services. And thanks to RLR Associates: Bob Rosen and Jennifer Unter.

Library of Congress Cataloging-in-Publication Data

Cullen, Bob.
  These guys are good / Bob Cullen ; with Melanie Hauser ... [et al.].
    p. cm.
  ISBN 1-933208-00-7 (hardcover : alk. paper)
  1.  Golf--Tournaments--United States--Anecdotes. 2.  Golfers--Anecdotes. 3.  PGA Tour (Association)  I. Hauser, Melanie. II. Title.
  GV970.C85 2005
  796.352'64--dc22

                                                    2004027834

Tehabi Books offers special discounts for bulk purchases of *These Guys are Good.* Copies may be used for corporate hospitality, sales promotions, and/or premium items. Specific needs can be met with customized covers, letter inserts, single-copy mailing cartons with a corporate imprint, and the repurposing of materials into new editions. For more information, contact Andrew Arias, Corporate Sales Manager, Tehabi Books, 4920 Carroll Canyon Road, Suite 200, San Diego, California 92121-3735; 1-800-243-7259.

In the United States, trade bookstores and other book retailers may contact Advantage Publishers Group for sales and distribution information at 1-858-457-2500. Specialty golf retailers may contact The Booklegger for sales and distribution information at 1-800-262-1556.

In Canada, *These Guys are Good* is distributed by Georgetown Publications, Inc., 34 Armstrong Avenue, Georgetown, ON L7G 4R9 CANADA (1-888-595-3008).

Printed in Verona, Italy by Editoriale Bortolazzi-Stei. Tehabi is proud to partner with EBS in the printing and binding of this and other titles in the PGA TOUR Publishing Program. Printed on 150gsm Gardamatt.

10 9 8 7 6 5 4 3 2 1

p.4
Vijay Singh became the world's number one golfer in 2004.
p.6
Sergio Garcia fires from the rough beside the fans in 2003.
p.8
Tiger Woods celebrates victory at the 2001 Bay Hill Invitational.
p.10
Fans watch the Buick Invitational from all angles at Torrey Pines.
p.12
Phil Mickelson wins his first major—the 2004 Masters.
p.16
2004 Masters Champion Phil Mickelson and his fans

foreword

by PHIL MICKELSON

16

· · · ·

CHAPTER 1

a story in every shot

by BOB CULLEN

20

· · · ·

CHAPTER 2

an inner fire

by MELANIE HAUSER

64

· · · ·

CHAPTER 3

a sense of place

by DAVID BARRETT

102

· · · ·

CHAPTER 4

the legacy of greatness

by BOB CULLEN

144

· · · ·

CHAPTER 5

reaching beyond limits

by MARK SOLTAU

180

We've all seen the interview that may seem a little awkward. It comes when the player walks off the last green headed for the scoring tent and the on-course commentator rushes up as time expires in the broadcast to ask what the win means to the young man. The answer most often is, "Well, it hasn't really sunk in yet." And a lot of viewers probably think, "What do you mean? You just won a two-year exemption and a million dollars!"

But this is what the player means by "it hasn't really sunk in yet." He means he hasn't had time to savor all the work he's put into getting that win or put behind him all the near misses he's had. He hasn't started to think about following his father up fairways as a kid or the college coach who encouraged him when things were tough or the wife and family who have been with him through thick and thin. He simply doesn't yet understand how much this means to him and to everyone who cares about him.

Playing on the PGA TOUR, let alone winning and being the best player in all of golf that day, is hard work, and the best players are so focused on the work they don't think about the outcome until after play is finished. There is the trophy presentation, the time spent with the volunteers and the committee, the media responsibilities— a lot happens quickly to a winner and it takes awhile to focus on what he's just accomplished. But that's all part of being a successful TOUR player.

One thing about golf is that every shot counts equally. A bogey on the first hole of the week is just as costly as one on the last hole. In between, there are hundreds of decisions to be made and dozens of distractions to be avoided. The pressure can be real or it can be imagined but it has to be dealt with, whether a player is trying to shoot 59, make the cut, or win the tournament.

In the pages that follow, written by some of the most thoughtful writers and enhanced by some of the best photographers in our game, I think you'll come to understand a lot more about what goes into playing on the PGA TOUR. Take your time. Let it sink in.

*Phil Mickelson*

"They hit shots that leave shots I could

me in awe,
only dream of."

LOU HALON,
PGA TOUR FAN
Raynham, Maryland

# a story
# in every
# shot

by
BOB CULLEN

PHIL MICKELSON

It was a Sunday sound at the 2004 Masters. As Phil Mickelson walked slowly toward the tee of the 12th hole he heard a roar rising near the azaleas around the 13th hole, bouncing among the pines at Amen Corner and carrying over the entire Augusta National Golf Club. He knew immediately what it meant. Ahead of him, Ernie Els had eagled the 13th.

## Mickelson now trailed by three strokes.

As he set his ball on the tee, the left-hander knew he had arrived at a place and a time that demanded a great shot. The flagstick on the 12th hole was where it usually is on Sunday, near the right edge of the wide, shallow green. That's the side where Rae's Creek cuts closest to the putting surface. It's the side where enigmatic breezes can turn even a good shot into a disaster. It's the side that conventional wisdom says you never aim at if you want to win the Masters.

Mickelson lugged some baggage onto the tee with him that day. In more than forty attempts, he had never won a major championship. Frequently, his critics said, he'd tossed away his chances by playing recklessly. From the start of the 2004 season he'd tried to play more conservatively, and that strategy had gotten him into the final pairing on Sunday. But now yet another major was slipping from his grasp.

There was something else Mickelson brought to the 12th tee: a new shot. Through the off-season and the first months of 2004, he'd worked to perfect a controlled fade, a shot that promised more control in return for less distance. It was a compromise the younger Mickelson had disdained but the new, more mature Mickelson welcomed.

# Great shots are made so not just by the stroke itself, but by the circumstances.

Now, the mature Mickelson joined forces with the risk-taking Mickelson. He took dead aim at the flagstick, 155 yards away. He calculated that if his shot drifted away from the flag, it would drift no more than a few yards toward the center of the green. He took his stance. Marshals gestured for absolute silence. Thousands of necks craned, thousands of eyes peered, all waiting to see if Mickelson could produce what the moment demanded for his survival—a great shot.

Just what makes a great shot?

To begin with, no one hits a great golf shot on Tuesday. You can see a multitude of impressive shots if you visit a PGA TOUR venue on a Tuesday. You'll see drives that rattle the fence at the end of the range, three hundred yards away. You'll see iron shots that home in on the flagstick as if it were a magnet. You'll see players dropping twenty-foot putt after curling, twenty-foot putt. But these are merely perfectly struck golf balls. They're not great shots. Great shots require something that a Tuesday practice session cannot provide. Great shots involve drama, tension, and gripping stories.

The *pok* of Mickelson's iron against the ball broke the silence. The crowd began a murmur. The ball hung in the air as if it had shed gravity, fell through a bit of wind, faded over the flag, and dropped onto the green twelve feet left of the cup. The gallery—Mickelson's gallery now—sent a roar down the course that Mickelson knew Els could hear as he teed up his own shot at the 14th. It was a great shot, a shot that Mickelson, clad in green a couple of hours later, would call the pivotal moment in his first major championship victory.

No one hits a
great golf shot
on a Tuesday.

Mickelson concentrates during the
2003 Buick Invitational.

**JOHN DALY**

watches his putt drop on the
72nd hole of the 1991 PGA
Championship. Daly won the title
after getting into the tournament
as an alternate and driving
all night to the site.

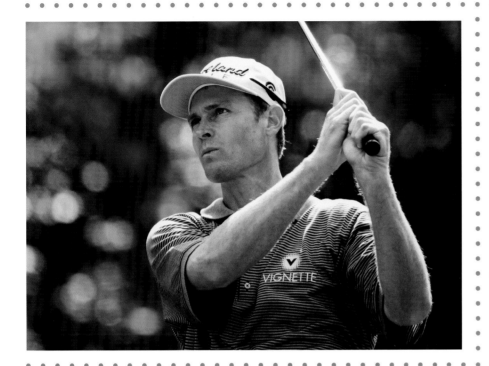

# To be great, a shot must be struck when the stakes are high.

Bob Estes hits an iron during the 2003 PLAYERS Championship on The Stadium Course at the Tournament Players Club at Sawgrass.

Great shots are made so not just by the stroke, but by the circumstances.

Ask Bob Estes to recall the greatest shot of his career and he recalls not one, but four. "Four times I've had to par the last hole to win. The first was the Texas Open in 1994. I had a 5-iron into a small, par-3 green and I hit it right in the center of the green and two-putted and won. The other three times I basically had to do the same thing. I hit perfect approach shots every single time. I did exactly what I was trying to do with every approach shot."

None of those four shots went in the hole. None even stopped close enough to the hole for an easy birdie. All would have been unremarkable on a Tuesday. Yet, to Estes, they are his greatest. "It has to do with doing it under pressure. I've made holes-in-one, I've made great pitch-ins or bunker shots or long putts or whatever, but the shots that really mean the most are the ones you do under pressure to win a golf tournament," he explains.

That's the essence of it. To be great, a shot needs a context, a story. To be great, a shot must be struck when the stakes are high, when a golfer confronts the possibility of realizing a cherished dream as well as seeing it evaporate. It ought to come at a turning point in a championship on the TOUR.

The great shot sweeps us up in its drama. When a great shot is struck, you can almost hear "Yes!" coming from television viewers in sports bars, living rooms, and dormitory lounges across the country.

It helps if the shot is struck on a course imbued with the memories of past dramas and past heroes. It ought to come on a hole that demands precision and penalizes the slightest error. The shot should be planned boldly, by a player who considers safer routes and realizes that playing safely will not get the job done.

Luck and great shots are almost incompatible. Luck plays an inextricable role in golf, even adds to the charm of the game. But great shots are not the ones that unexpectedly carom off tree limbs or roll through bunkers and into the hole. They're shots that come off the way the golfer planned them.

Finally, a great shot is often the climax of a great personal story, a story replete with setbacks and struggles, a story of bravery and redemption.

The archetype may be the 1-iron hit by Ben Hogan to the 18th green at Merion Golf Club during the final round of the 1950 U.S. Open. On the face of it, it was nothing more than a 220-yard approach shot that stopped forty feet from the hole and led to a two-putt par. But to say that would be to ignore the context.

It was the national championship. It was at Merion, a storied course on which Bobby Jones, twenty years earlier, had completed the Grand Slam. It was a daunting hole, a long par-4 requiring a drive over an old quarry and a long-iron approach, the traditional final test of a champion's nerve and skill.

A great shot is often the climax of a great personal story.

After his accident, Ben Hogan returned to golf at the 1950 Los Angeles Open, but he lost to Sam Snead in a playoff.

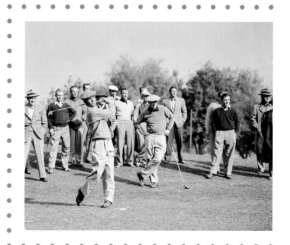

**BEN HOGAN**
hits his decisive 1-iron shot
toward the 18th green at the
1950 U.S. Open. This is one of
golf's most famous photographs.

"Anyone can handle victory but the real measure of a person is how he handles

STEPHEN THOMPSON,
PGA TOUR FAN
Citrus Heights, California

Robert Allenby of Australia reacts to a putt that he barely missed on the
17th green during singles play at the 2003 Presidents Cup in South Africa.
Allenby got up and won the next hole to halve his match with Davis Love III.

defeat."

BEN HOGAN
celebrates shooting a final round
of 67 at Detroit's Oakland Hills
to win the 1951 U.S. Open.

Most important, the shot was made by a man who, only fourteen months before, had had a **head-on collision with a Greyhound bus.** Hogan had thrown himself across the seat of his car to protect his wife, Valerie. The steering column had fractured his left collarbone. The engine had broken through the car's firewall, fracturing his left ankle, mangling his left leg, and breaking his pelvis. The notion that Hogan would ever again play competitive golf had seemed preposterous.

But he had come back, displaying the same tenacity and singleness of purpose that he had brought to learning the game. Hogan was renowned for the hours of practice he devoted to the game. He became equally renowned for the gritty way he rehabilitated himself. His injuries did not fully heal. Just to get around the golf course, Hogan had to adopt a tortuous preparatory routine that included soaking in hot water and Epsom salts, swallowing aspirin, rubbing on liniment, and, finally, wrapping his legs like a mummy's.

In those days, Open contestants played thirty-six holes on the final day, called "Open Saturday." Hogan's legs lasted about thirteen before they seized up. But he did not quit. **He dragged himself around the course.** His caddie picked his ball from the cup. His playing partner, Dr. Cary Middlecoff, marked his ball for him. **He was testing the limits of endurance** and resistance to pain when he came to the final hole. Then he struck that perfect 1-iron. It was a triumph of will—a great shot.

The great shot sweeps us up in its drama.

Ben Hogan tees off at Baltusrol in the 1954 U.S. Open, unsuccessfully seeking his fifth title.

# What emerge from the crucible are both great shots and great stories.

Shots like that are still struck on the PGA TOUR and savored by those who understand the stories behind them. Take, for instance, the shots that David Toms hit to take the 2001 PGA Championship from Mickelson. Toms, on the 18th hole at the Atlanta Athletic Club, had a lie difficult in the rough and more than two hundred yards to go to the green, the last part over water. He knew that even if he cleared the hazard with a 3-iron or 5-wood shot, he wouldn't be able to stop the ball on the green and would face a difficult chip toward the water from thick grass.

So Toms did the wise thing. He laid up to lob-wedge distance, put his next shot ten feet from the hole, and made the putt, winning the tournament. All three of his final shots on the hole were great ones, because all were struck under intense pressure. All three did what Toms wanted them to do. And all three were evidence of judgment and grace under pressure.

Great shots demand great judgment, in addition to great skill.

That's what the PGA TOUR elicits, week after week. It's a crucible in which golfers mix the elements of high stakes, great courses, and big crowds. It forces the players to reach deep within themselves, and what emerge from the crucible are both great shots and great stories.

**DAVID TOMS**
won the 2001 PGA Championship
by laying up short of a pond
on the final hole, pitching on,
and sinking this par putt.

Todd Hamilton (left), ranked fifty-sixth in the world going into the tournament, leaps into
the arms of his caddie, Ron Levin, after winning the 2004 British Open against number two-ranked
Ernie Els. Tiger Woods (above) is alone in his anguish at the 2001 Bay Hill Invitational.

# "Nobody out there cares who's when you tee it up."

VIJAY SINGH

Vijay Singh became the world's top-ranked player in 2004.

Number 1

PAUL AZINGER
watches another of his perfect
bunker shots.

# Part of the game

Great golf shots that linger in memory often have an emotional subtext. Such was the bunker shot with which Paul Azinger defeated Payne Stewart in the 1993 Memorial Tournament.

It was an emotional shot as well for those who knew how close Stewart and Azinger were. They were contemporaries, fishing buddies, and young fathers together. They were best friends.

Stewart came to the 72nd hole of the tournament with a one-shot lead over Azinger. Both hit 1-irons off the tee and encountered misfortune. Azinger's shot lit on a soft spot in the fairway and sat 212 yards from the green. Stewart's shot rolled out well ahead of Azinger's but came to rest in a sand-filled divot. Azinger hit into a greenside bunker that was six feet deep, and he had a moment of despair. "I can't win this tournament," he thought. Then Stewart's approach landed in the same bunker. It bored into the sand, leaving him a fried-egg lie.

Stewart managed to hack his ball out to eight feet, a brilliant shot given his lie. Azinger began to apply all the things he had taught himself about bunker play. He closed his eyes and visualized the shot he wanted. Then he pulled his sand wedge and stepped into the bunker.

He set himself and swung as hard as he could, trying to impart some backspin to the ball. It popped up, barely clearing the lip. It hit the green and the backspin checked it. The ball began to trickle toward the hole, rolling like a teardrop down a cheek, breaking left. In the bunker, Azinger sagged back onto his knees, arms thrust up, watching the ball roll, turn, and finally topple into the cup. The enormous crowd in the natural amphitheater around the last green at Muirfield Village Golf Club erupted in cheers.

Stewart, stunned, missed his par putt and the championship belonged to his good friend. Azinger had tears in his eyes even before he stepped out of the sand, tears of both elation and compassion.

"Payne, I am really sorry," he said.

"It's okay, bud," Stewart replied. "That's part of it. That's the game."

As Azinger accepted the trophy and the winner's check, Stewart retired to the locker room, where he had a cold drink with tournament chairman Pandel Savic. Then he got some bananas, mashed them up, and stuffed them into Azinger's street shoes.

More than a decade later, and years after Stewart's death in a plane crash, Azinger finds that his memories of the shot have only grown more lustrous, thanks to the valor, grace, and humor that Stewart displayed.

"It was a unique moment," Azinger says. "He handled it so well."

Payne Stewart handles a sand trap during the 1993 AT&T Pebble Beach National Pro-Am.

"The players sometimes make the same that I often do."

GENE WEIGANT,
PGA TOUR FAN
Jacksonville, Florida

Jerry Kelly vents his frustration with his putt on the
14th hole at the 2003 Presidents Cup.

mistakes

**ROBERT DAMRON**
three-putted and lost his playoff
with Sergio Garcia for the 2004
EDS Byron Nelson Championship.

# If I had it to do over...

For every triumph there is a tragedy, and for every great shot there is another that a player would love to have over. But doing it over is not part of golf. Once struck, there is no replaying a shot that didn't work—no mulligan. That's why golf tournaments are so dramatic. A player gets one chance at a critical shot and either succeeds or fails.

If you ask PGA TOUR players about the shots they'd most like to play over, an unexpected pattern emerges. Often it's not the swing they'd like to reprise; it's the thinking that led to the swing.

Robert Damron lost the 2004 EDS Byron Nelson Championship in a playoff to Sergio Garcia, missing a four-foot par putt on the final hole. But it's not the putt he'd like to do over; it's the 5-iron he hit to the green. "I hit a bad 5-iron because I wasn't comfortable with the club," he recalls, "and I flared it to the right. I set myself up to three-putt. If I had it to do over, I'd hit a hard 6-iron."

Loren Roberts had similar thoughts about the 8-iron he hit to the 72nd green of the 1994 U.S. Open. Needing a par to win, Roberts hit a perfect drive. "I was in between clubs and I played it back in my stance and tried to hit a lower shot in there," he remembers, "and it hit just on the portion of the green in the middle where there's a hollow, like a ditch. It hit the downslope and skipped through into the back fringe and I ended up not getting it up and down." Roberts lost in the playoff the next day to Ernie Els. "If I had it to do over," he says, "I'd play a higher, softer shot."

Players remember shots gone bad in critical situations, but the setting isn't always a major championship. Tripp Isenhour hit a shot to the island green 14th on the Silver Course at Doral during the 1998 PGA TOUR Qualifying Tournament, and he still remembers it. "I hit a 9-iron to a back pin even though I thought the lie might give me a flyer," he recalls. "It flew the green and went in the water. I made double-bogey and missed getting my card by two strokes. I should have hit a wedge and gone for the middle of the green."

The memories can linger for a lifetime. "The shot I'd like to have over again is a three-foot putt I missed to lose the Kemper Open in 1983, the year Fred Couples won his first event," says Scott Simpson. "I wouldn't mind taking a stab at that putt again. I'd play it a little higher now that I have the read."

Such memories can be painful, but the missed shot does serve one positive function. It acts the way a foil of base metal acts in the setting of a diamond ring. It reminds us that nothing is easy or routine on the PGA TOUR. It suggests how special great shots truly are.

Ireland's Padraig Harrington reacts after missing a putt at the 2004 Barclays Classic.

TIGER WOODS

makes a recovery shot from
the rough in the midst of
an avid gallery in 2003.

# Shot of a lifetime

Scott McCarron fires an iron during the Nissan Open.

On the PGA TOUR, great shots are always a little magical. Sometimes the magic is visible; other times it's in the mind of the player.

Matt Kuchar recalls the drive he hit to the 18th fairway during the final round of the 2002 Honda Classic, his first victory on the TOUR. It was special to him because he knew he was in contention at the time and knew what he had to do. The fairway was guarded by water down the right side and sand on the left. Kuchar had hit into a bunker in all three previous rounds.

Faced with the formidable pressure of trying to win his first tournament, Kuchar stepped up and hit precisely the tee shot he wanted, a ball that started toward the bunkers on the left, then faded into the fairway. From that point, he knew he could close out the tournament.

"There were big crowds, but there wasn't much reaction," Kuchar recalls. "To them it was just a drive. But there was a lot of excitement in my mind."

Playing in the 1994 Bay Hill Invitational, Loren Roberts hit a weak tee shot on the 18th hole in the third round. He faced an intimidating approach to a shallow green, with the last 140 yards entirely over water. He hit a 3-wood that soared dead straight on the line he'd chosen and wound up about 18 feet from the hole. Roberts made the putt for a birdie, and that shot gave him the confidence and momentum he needed to claim his first tournament win the next day.

But it was not a shot many of his fans remember. "I was in the last or next-to-last group, and it was getting late," he says. "The telecast had ended. Nobody really saw the shot." But Roberts hasn't forgotten it. "From that far back, I could've made anything on the hole. I just caught it dead perfect."

Sometimes, on the other hand, a player's greatest shot is a thrill for everyone present. Scott McCarron's was struck at the 1999 CVS Charity Classic, the two-day fundraising event organized by Brad Faxon and Billy Andrade.

McCarron was playing in a group that included Lee Janzen. On the 17th hole, a short par-3, Janzen made a hole-in-one. McCarron was seized by a premonition. "I told Lee to get his ball out of the hole because I was going to make one on top of him," he says. "I hit a 9-iron and it lit just past the hole and spun back a foot into the cup. The spectators were falling out of the bleachers. Tim Herron, my partner, was rolling on the ground. It was the greatest shot I ever hit because I knew it was going to happen."

And sometimes a player's favorite shot isn't even struck in competition. "My favorite shot? A 1-iron, 150 yards, off the back of an alligator," recalls Paul Azinger. "I was at home, playing with my brother. I saw a gator lying by a pond with a golf ball on his back. I said to my brother, 'Watch this.' I was in a cart and I drove up, jumped out, and hit the shot. The gator did a 180-degree turn and landed in the water."

MATT KUCHAR
is satisfied with the final tee shot
of his first championship, at the
2002 Honda Classic.

**ARNOLD PALMER** watches a putt miss in the last round of the 1962 Masters. After this shot, he tumbled to 3-over-par, but recovered with birdies on the 16th and 17th holes to force a three-way playoff with Gary Player and Dow Finsterwald, which Palmer won.

SCOTT McCARRON
wins the 2001 BellSouth Classic.
The tournament has contributed more
than $10 million to its primary charity,
Children's Healthcare of Atlanta.

# The biggest TOUR victories

For the PGA TOUR it's simple: giving back makes things better. Whether it's a teenager learning life values in the Big Apple, an inner-city youth attending a progressive school in Texas, or the daughter of a deceased military officer receiving much-needed funds to attend college, thousands are touched each year by the PGA TOUR's contributions to charity.

At nearly every tournament, the PGA TOUR donates the net proceeds to charity. The EDS Byron Nelson Classic, which in 2004 alone raised over $6 million in net proceeds, is the biggest giver, with other tournaments, such as the FedEx St. Jude and THE PLAYERS Championship, running close behind. Altogether, since the first $10,000 was raised in 1938 at the Palm Beach Invitational, the total amount of money donated to charity by the PGA TOUR, Champions Tour, and Nationwide Tour over the past six decades will soon top $1 billion.

The tournaments are able to give so much because of the dedicated efforts of the thousands of staff members and volunteers who work to make the events possible.

Yet it is not only the tournaments that give. Many individual players, including Tiger Woods, Phil Mickelson, and David Toms, have created their own foundations to benefit others and the communities they live in.

For instance, when Phil Mickelson sinks an eagle or birdie putt, it means that hours, days, or weeks of practice have paid off for him. It also means a payoff for his Birdies for the Brave program, which contributes to the Special Operations Warrior Foundation (SOWF), which in turn pays educational expenses for children of Special Operations soldiers killed in the line of duty. Those contributions mean Stephanie Matos is able to study for a degree in physical therapy at the University of South Florida on a SOWF grant. "They handed me a future," Stephanie says, "and I realized that I could be a lot more than I was giving myself credit for."

For those associated with the PGA TOUR, the money raised each year for so many worthy causes is a reminder that many TOUR victories are earned off the course.

"The Warrior Foundation has changed I would not be the person I am today without them."

STEPHANIE MATOS,
WARRIOR FOUNDATION
SCHOLARSHIP RECIPIENT

Every time he makes a birdie or an eagle, Phil Mickelson contributes scholarship money to the Warrior Foundation through his Birdies for the Brave program.

# Bunker magic

David Frost, whose bunker play has won him championships, in the sand at the 2004 Barclays Classic at Westchester Country Club.

Ah, the sand.

Few of the great shots on the PGA TOUR dazzle fans the way that great bunker shots do. Maybe that's because the average golfer dreads bunker shots when he's on the course himself. He calls the bunker a sand trap, and for him it truly is.

For the players on the PGA TOUR, the sand is a friendly medium—it doesn't bother them any more than straitjackets bothered Houdini. Indeed, there's something Houdini-like about the way they get out.

When David Frost holed a greenside bunker shot to beat Greg Norman in New Orleans in 1990, he was the least-surprised person among the throng around the final green at English Turn Golf and Country Club. Frost was tied with Norman when he came to the tee of that long, perilous par-4. His drive into a fairway bunker wasn't intentional. Good as they are from sand, TOUR players prefer fairway grass.

Frost considered his options and decided that he would rather flirt with the lake and the big bunker left of the 18th green than miss his shot to the right. No one had been getting the ball up and down from the right. His second shot missed the green, but it found the left greenside bunker. What would terrify the typical amateur comforted Frost. "I had a perfect lie, eighty feet from the hole. I saw a pitch mark on the green where I intended to land the ball, and I went and fixed it," Frost recalls. "The ball landed right on that spot. It released and trickled into the hole. I was in the last group and it was the last shot. It worked exactly as I'd planned, though I had planned to get it close, make par, and get into a playoff. Instead, I won by a stroke." Tiger Woods did not win the 2000 Canadian Open with the fairway bunker shot he played on the last hole. He still had to make a couple of putts. But it was Woods's audacity from the sand that the fans remember.

Woods, running a stroke ahead of Grant Waite of New Zealand, drove his ball into a fairway bunker 218 yards from the hole, a par-5. Not only did he face a sandy lie; the route to the green ran over a lake. Woods pulled his 6-iron and, in the eyes of many fans, gambled.

He clipped the ball cleanly out of the bunker. The ball rose over the right side of the fairway and kept rising until it was almost lost among the gray clouds spitting a drizzle onto Glen Abbey Golf Club. As it descended, the crowd's buzz grew to a roar. The ball landed about eighteen feet behind the hole and settled in the first cut of rough. It was one of the boldest and best bunker shots in history, securing the Triple Crown for Woods that summer—the U.S., British, and Canadian Opens.

But when it was over, Woods himself didn't seem to consider the shot remarkable. "When pressure is at its peak, that's when your concentration level is at its highest," he said. "It builds to a crescendo."

Just like the roar of the crowd.

TIGER WOODS
demonstrates the technique
that makes sand play a strong
part of his game.

The difference between triumph and tragedy can be measured in inches. Ernie Els (left)
sinks a birdie putt to win the playoff at the 2003 Sony Open. Aaron Baddeley (above)
barely missed the putt he needed to match him.

LARRY MIZE
becomes a Masters champion by
sinking a birdie chip on the second
playoff hole in 1987.

# Holing it

You can have your Hail Mary passes, your half-court buzzer-beaters, and your one-punch knockouts. For audacity, skill, and shocking surprise, there is nothing in sport to rival a swift coup de grâce that decides a tournament.

Such shots occur rarely. When they do, they instantly become memories cherished both by the players who struck them and the fans who saw them.

Sometimes, the winning shot is the result of planning. As often as not, there's some luck involved as well. Larry Mize was just "chipping to get it close," but his 140-foot bump-and-run found the cup on the 11th hole of the Augusta National and decided his playoff with Greg Norman in the 1987 Masters Tournament.

Skill played the greater role. "I walked up to the green to look at the firmness of the ground, then check the spot where I wanted the ball to land. I felt like anything that landed on the green would be too hard. I was nervous, but one of the nice things about it was there was no indecision. There was only one shot I felt I could play. I took a sand wedge, played the ball back in my stance, and bumped it into the fringe. It felt good from the moment it left the club face."

The ball broke several feet from right to left and rolled in. As it did, Larry Mize's life changed. The shot made him a Masters champion.

What does such a shot feel like? Craig Parry could barely find the words after he holed a 6-iron on the first playoff hole to beat Scott Verplank at the Ford Championship at Doral in 2004. "The crowd went absolutely nuts," he recalled later. "Obviously, it was in the hole. It all went pretty quick."

Parry, too, was trying to get the shot close. He wasn't thinking about holing it. The outcome was almost as much a shock to him as it was to Verplank.

Getting it close was all Robert Gamez was trying to do when he holed a 7-iron from 176 yards on the 18th hole to win the 1990 Bay Hill Invitational. Gamez was nervous before he hit the shot, and his nerves indirectly helped him. He was thinking of hitting a soft, cut 6-iron to the green. But when he's nervous, he likes to hit the ball hard. So he took his 7-iron.

The ball flew a shade right of the flag, then rode the wind as it bit left, hit the green, and hopped in. "I was shooting at the pin, but you never think it's going to go in," Gamez recalls. He remembers one more thing about his coup de grâce shot. "When I saw the ball go in, it was excitement," he says.

## "Pure excitment."

Mize blasts from a bunker earlier in the final round of the 1987 Masters.

JESPER PARNEVIK
and Sergio Garcia celebrate Parnevik's
winning shot in the Saturday four-ball
competition at the 1999 Ryder Cup.

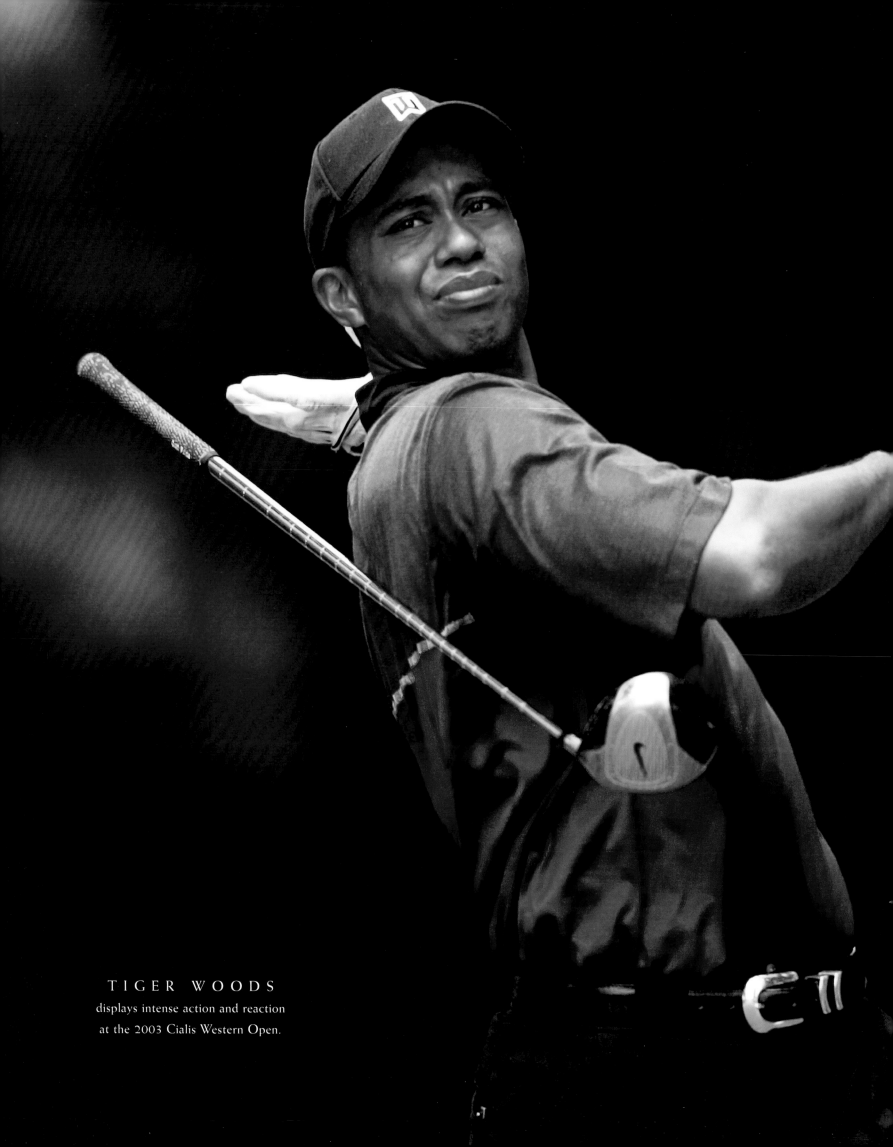

TIGER WOODS
displays intense action and reaction
at the 2003 Cialis Western Open.

# an inner fire

by

MELANIE HAUSER

**TIGER WOODS** shows his ability to concentrate even while under pressure with this shot at the 2004 Buick Invitational.

As the kid walked underneath the sprawling oak tree a few minutes before his tee time that Sunday afternoon in 1997, everyone standing there knew this was not just another final round. It was history.

The kid seemed oblivious to the people gathered on that famous lawn, the people whose conversations hushed in mid-word as he made his way to the putting green, where he could take a deep breath and make sure—one last time—his hands had the feel, the speed of those greens. He was focused on what was about to unfold.

Tiger Woods looked so young, so innocent, so confident. So lethal.

You wanted to get into his mind. You wanted to understand that steely focus. You wanted to inhabit his body, to feel the power of his swing. You wanted to know how it felt to make a ball dance onto a green and stop on a single blade of bentgrass. You wanted to know how a man could be so calmly dominant in his first major as a professional. You wondered what it must feel like to know you're playing eighteen holes not against another player, but against a number in a record book.

If ever a moment touched you, it was that one at the Masters Tournament. We were about to witness a coronation, a racial barrier being shattered, a defining moment in the game. A moment—and a twelve-shot victory—that awes us to this day.

## You want to get into his mind. You want to understand that steely focus.

Woods, only 22 at the time, amazed everyone with the drive and determination that led him to a twelve-shot win at his first major, the 1997 Masters.

What we saw that afternoon in Woods was a determination, a grace under such intense pressure, a performance that humbled a sport. We saw an inner fire.

Woods, of course, didn't stop at Augusta. Three years later, he won the U.S. Open at Pebble Beach by fifteen shots and completed the career Grand Slam a month later at the British Open at St. Andrews, winning by eight shots. It was during that run, after Pebble Beach, that Woods let us peek inside.

"There comes a point in time when you feel tranquil, when you feel calm; you feel at ease with yourself," Woods said of the double-digit wins at majors. "In those two weeks, I felt that way. I felt very at ease with myself. And for some reason, things just flowed. No matter what you do—good or bad—it really doesn't get to you. Even the days when you wake up on the wrong side of the bed, for some reason it doesn't feel too bad; it's just all right."

Tiger Woods's inner fire, his unwavering focus and belief in himself, attracts us as the sun attracts planets. We can't get enough of it. We want to know about the early days when his father, Earl, introduced him to the game, about his teenage years, about his amateur years. We want to know about the expectations—his, not ours—that have pushed him every step of his career.

And in having those expectations, he's not alone.

Woods, here at the 2000 U.S. Open, which he won by fifteen shots, gives his all to every shot he makes, every round he plays.

Every player on the PGA TOUR has that something special deep down inside.

**JESPER PARNEVIK**
shows the effort of his shot even after
the ball has flown at the second hole
of the Firestone Country Club during
the 2004 World Golf Championships-
NEC Invitational.

ALL

"You want to be there on Sunday, on the back nine, and that is you want to do."

CHRIS DiMARCO

Chris DiMarco celebrates a birdie putt during the
2004 Ryder Cup matches. The birdie helped him and Jay Haas defeat
Spain's Miguel Angel Jiminez and France's Thomas Levet.

**JAY HAAS**
lines up a putt at the 2003 World Golf
Championships-Accenture Match Play
Championship. He has improved his
performance at an age when most
players' careers are winding down.

# The game arouses something in them. They're driven to excel.

Rich Beem celebrates as a birdie putt goes down on his way to winning the 2002 PGA Championship, his first major.

Every player on the PGA TOUR has that something special deep down inside. The game arouses something in these players. They were tugged to pick it up as boys. They're driven to excel, all the while knowing that golf is a capricious and cruel sport where there exists the finest of lines between perfection rewarded and a heart ripped out.

And the fire? It can be as palpable as that of Tiger Woods during that run for the Slam or as quiet and efficient as Jay Haas, causing us to change our sense of when middle age begins. It can be as long-burning as Phil Mickelson's quest for a major. It can be as endless as a day on the range with Vijay Singh. It can't be wrapped up neatly with a ribbon. It's something different for everyone. It's daring to push limits—both conventional and personal. It's putting a bad hole, a bad season, or a dry spell in the majors out of your mind and concentrating on what's ahead.

"Every one of us has moments where we have doubts and we have to overcome them," Woods says. "That's part of the game. Part of the sport."

# It is about persistence and perseverance.

Mark O'Meara contemplates a putt at the 2004 Buick Open.

When a player does elevate his game and his focus, when he does do what, at times, no one but himself ever thought possible, it's a moment that touches everyone. Take Mark O'Meara. He could tear up Pebble Beach at the AT&T Pebble Beach National Pro-Am; he could win twenty times worldwide, but none of those victories was a major. He was 0-for-56 at the majors until 1998, when his perseverance finally paid off at the age of forty-one. In one magical year, he won the Masters and the British Open.

This is a man who revamped his swing early in his career and never gave up. He spent years washing his own car and saving money on the road by staying at inexpensive motels. He didn't worry about his receding hairline or his aching joints. When he got into position at the 1998 Masters, he went for it. He went to the final hole tied with Fred Couples and David Duval, then sank a twenty-foot, right-to-left birdie putt, thrust his arms into the air, and was swallowed in a bear hug from caddie Jerry Higgenbotham.

"I hit that putt a lot in the practice rounds," O'Meara says. "I said to myself, 'Look, this is what it's all about. This is why I play golf for a living. Am I nervous? Yeah, but there's no need to go into a playoff. I've got the tournament in my own hands. Let's finish it off.' And it went in the left center of the cup."

And, no, he couldn't describe the feeling.

For O'Meara, who went on to win the British Open at Birkdale later that year, beating Brian Watts in a playoff, it was all about persistence and perseverance.

MARK O'MEARA
tees off on the 12th hole
at the 1998 Masters.

SCOTT VERPLANK
has persevered to fashion a long
PGA TOUR career.

Scott Verplank would have to agree. He won his first PGA TOUR event in 1985—the Western Open—as an amateur. That win, in a playoff over Jim Thorpe, seemed to signal a fast track into the TOUR's elite. It didn't.

Verplank's career has been plagued by injuries and surgeries, and his PGA TOUR path has been anything but a rocket to the top. He has lost his card and his confidence, endured surgeries on both elbows, and pushed through strings of missed cuts (he made just one cut in 1991) while battling diabetes throughout his career. He never lost heart.

Verplank, long known as one of the grittiest players on the TOUR, has been forced to slow down at times, but he's rebounded time after time. That resilience prompted Curtis Strange. in 2002, to make Verplank the first rookie to be chosen as a captain's pick in U.S. Ryder Cup history.

"To come back mentally from something like that, those of us who have never gone through that will never know how tough that is," Strange says. "That's the toughest thing. Physically, you can overcome hurdles, but mentally to overcome something like that, to be so down on yourself and your golf game, shows a lot of intestinal fortitude."

Strange's other pick that season? Paul Azinger. Zinger, as he's known, is all about fire. He battled Seve Ballesteros in 1989 at The Belfry and didn't back down. Not long after he beat Greg Norman to win the 1993 PGA Championship, he was diagnosed with lymphoma in his shoulder. He battled the cancer and beat it.

"When I was in my second month of treatments, Johnny Miller told me, 'Zinger, it's not always what you accomplish in life that matters, but what you overcome,' " Azinger said.

Six years later he was one of those the golf world looked to when Payne Stewart and three other close friends of Azinger died in a plane crash. Zinger fought through it all a few months later and won the Sony Open in Hawaii—his first TOUR victory since 1993.

# It's not what you accomplish in life, it's what you overcome.

# Every time they step onto the course they're focused on winning.

Tom Kite, at the 1993 Bob Hope Chrysler Classic, is one of the players who demonstrates the connections between desire, practice, and success.

Inner fire is what fuels you. It could be endless hours on the range with Tom Kite. It could be **winning majors or making cuts.** It could be closing the deal coming down the stretch. It could be losing as graciously as you win—and turning those missed opportunities into wins the next time around.

It is drive, as in Tiger Woods's struggling through a swing change, putting problems, questions on top of questions, and still breaking Byron Nelson's record for consecutive cuts made—113—at the 2003 TOUR Championship.

Jack Nicklaus is the man we look to when it comes to majors. He won an amazing eighteen of them. But did you know he finished second nineteen times? He was tough. He was focused. He's still the greatest player who ever lived.

Tiger Woods once marveled at how he and Nicklaus—two different people from different eras; two men who don't see much of each other—could feel so close. Every time they step onto the course they're focused on winning, on what they want to accomplish.

# It's what drives them to be the best.

JACK NICKLAUS
won two of his three Claret Jugs
at St. Andrews, the home of golf,
including this one in 1975.

**MIKE WEIR**
played for years on minor tours until he became a member of the PGA TOUR and a champion. Weir's victories include THE TOUR Championship in 2001 and The Masters in 2003.

# Perseverance

Tom Lehman escapes from a bunker at THE TOUR Championship in 1996, the season he led the money list.

It sounds like a legend, but it's true: Tom Lehman did indeed once shower in the rain. He was on the road, grimy and down to his last few dollars. He didn't want to spend those on a hotel. So he stepped out of his car in a storm and cleaned up.

Ah, the glamour of mini-tours! The long drives. Sharing rooms with buddies or caddies. Breakfast or dinner at mom-and-pop diners. Keeping an eye out for snakes in Asia. Missing family while you're in South Africa. All with one goal in mind: making it to golf's big show, the PGA TOUR.

Lehman worked his way up the ladder, rung by rung. He made the TOUR in the early 1980s, but he lost his card. He turned down the coaching job at the University of Minnesota, his alma mater, because he didn't want to sell snow skis out of the pro shop during the winter.

His inner fire kept him going. He played every tour imaginable—from the Hooters to the Dakotas to the T.C. Jordan, Golden State, and Space Coast. Players' entry fees made up the bulk of the purses on those tours, so playing in them was a form of gambling—on yourself.

"You had to win to survive," he says. "That taught me a lot about golf and a lot about myself."

It taught him enough to win the British Open and THE TOUR Championship and lead the money list in 1996. Enough to—for the week of April 20, 1997—grab the No. 1 ranking in the world from Greg Norman. Sweet? We may never know just how sweet.

Lehman has never shied away from talking about the tough times. He's called them humiliating and frustrating. When he was playing in Memphis one day during that time, he missed a birdie putt at the 16th—a putt he needed in order to make the cut and cash a check that week. He was so mad he kicked a gallery rope and got his foot caught. Then he kicked a trash can, and his foot stayed in the can.

"It kind of summed up my whole story," he says. "I couldn't even get getting mad right that year. I think a real turning point came with me because I realized that I wanted to play golf not for the money anymore, but because I wanted to be good."

Lehman's work ethic and inner fire pushed him to the upper tier of players in the 1990s, and he never backed down. He is confident, patient, and tough, always looking for his next chance.

"I don't think I lost it," he said after the 1998 Open. "I didn't win it."

He understood that it just hadn't happened, and he hasn't stopped playing like it will.

TOM LEHMAN
reacts after his long par putt sneaks
into the hole at the 2003 AT&T
Pebble Beach National Pro-Am.

# "All I know is
# I hit it and it went

HANK KUEHNE

pretty
good."

Some players show emotion and some don't. Jim Furyk (above) was focused as he
worked his way to victory at the 2003 U.S. Open. Sergio Garcia (right) was expressive
after a missed putt that cost him the 2001 TOUR Championship.

**VIJAY SINGH**
holds a small towel under his left
arm to force him to keep the arm
close to his body as he swings.
Singh works unrelentingly
on drills like this during
practice sessions.

# Seeking perfection

### Vijay Singh doesn't know when to quit.

Just ask his caddie. Ask other players. Ask tournament directors who have been known to erect temporary lights on their driving ranges just in case. Singh opens ranges. He closes them down. His is not the hit-your-basic-bucket-of-balls-and-be-done-with-it routine.

Singh is after one thing—perfection. Don't ask him to put a time limit on it. He has made a career out of hard work and silence. He shuts out the world and focuses on one ball at a time, on making it do exactly what he wants every time he hits it. "The harder I work," he says, "I feel I can win more and more."

If Ben Hogan invented practice, Singh is close to perfecting it. He goes to the far end of the range anytime he can to find the peace and solitude he needs. Give him a couple of hundred balls and watch him pick apart each swing. Singh's practice sessions, which call to mind Hogan's and those of the young Tom Kite, are legendary.

He works primarily in solitude, but Singh also finds a quiet camaraderie on the range, often at twilight, with peers who are also bent on seeking perfection. He teaches. He even jokes and laughs, delighting in the fellowship of the striver. He seems to understand that when he offers instruction, he's learning, too.

Tiger Woods conveyed the respect Singh's practice has earned from his peers when he told the story of finding a six-foot-long, three-foot-wide bunker during a practice round at Whistling Straits prior to the 2004 PGA Championship. "Looks like Vijay has been here," he chuckled.

Ah, yes. The players know Singh's practice signature—long divots and lots of them. Singh is always tinkering with his swing, with his putter, with his putting stroke. The ultimate justification is in his record. He's won a Masters and two PGA Championships. He won the money title in 2003. In late summer of 2004 he became the world's number-one player in the midst of one of the best seasons in PGA TOUR history. In his early forties, he's working on a Hall of Fame career.

Singh's 2004 PGA Championship—his first major title in four years—wasn't pretty. In fact, it was downright ugly. He didn't hit the shots he wanted and closed with a 76, just enough to put him into a playoff. He dipped into the well of skill he's dug for himself on the practice range and produced a perfect tee shot, smoked to within a few paces of the green on a 361-yard par-4. From there, a deft wedge and a five-foot putt gave him the edge he needed to beat Justin Leonard and Chris DiMarco.

"This win came at the right time," says Singh, who played the remaining two playoff holes in rock-solid par. "It's come at a stage of my life where I worked really hard and it's paying off. I've wanted something to happen in my career, and this is the start. I'm not stopping here. I'd like to win a few more before I finish. I think there's many more out there, I hope."

Vijay Singh responds to adversity by working harder.

TIGER WOODS
shows his determination at the
British Open in 1999, a year in which
he became the first player to win
four consecutive starts since
Ben Hogan in 1953.

**JUSTIN LEONARD**
reacts when his improbable birdie
putt goes in on the 17th hole
at the 1999 Ryder Cup.

# The incredible comeback

Fully focused at a critical moment, Leonard strikes the 45-foot putt that decided the 1999 Ryder Cup matches.

A single tear trickled down his cheek, then another. It was so uncharacteristic. Justin Leonard, a man known for his strength and composure, a man known as one of the best comeback players in the game, was on the edge—down by four with eight holes to play and trying desperately to pull himself together and get back into the match.

The 1999 Ryder Cup was slipping away. That hurt even more than the words of NBC's Johnny Miller the day before, when Miller said that Leonard should have stayed home and watched the matches on television.

As Leonard approached the 11th tee, Davis Love III walked up and grabbed Leonard by the shoulders. Love looked Leonard straight in the eye and told him his teammates believed in him. It wasn't over. He could turn this one around.

Four down with eight to play? He'd come from that far down against David Duval in his 1992 U.S. Amateur win, hadn't he? He'd come from seven shots back to win three times—the 1997 Kemper and British Opens and the 1998 PLAYERS Championship—right? Why not do it again? Why not do it here?

"I had that thought with me," he recalled later. "I knew it was possible."

Leonard halved the next hole. Then he dug deep, found the magic, and lifted the American team on his shoulders. He won the 12th hole. He won the 13th. He won the 14th. He sank a 35-footer at the 15th to square the match.

Suddenly, this match wasn't just for him. It was for the 11 other guys on this team and for captain Ben Crenshaw. It was for the United States, which was staging the greatest comeback in Ryder Cup history.

Two holes later, Leonard's approach to the 17th green had too much spin on it. It just missed catching the top tier and spun back to 45 feet. José Maria Olazabal was 30 feet away. Neither shot was a gimme two-putt.

Then Leonard did what he does best. He lined up his putt and took dead aim. It charged up the hill, crested it, and dove right into the hole. Leonard opened his arms and ran across the green, looking for someone to hug. The team erupted. It was pandemonium.

As it turned out, Leonard didn't win a match all week. He went 0-0-3. But with that last draw, with that incredible comeback, he not only lifted himself up from the lowest point in his golf career, he carried the team on his shoulders.

When it was over, when Leonard was standing with the team celebrating at The Country Club, he couldn't help but be proud of what he had accomplished on a brilliant back nine, proud of how he had turned his match and the fortunes of his team around, proud of proving Miller and a few others wrong.

"I think," Leonard says with that steely stare of his, "it was a good thing I didn't go home."

"I am a fan of the underdog, the longshot, the grinder, and the that even the 300th-ranked player in the world can win."

ED SORGE,
PGA TOUR FAN
New York, New York

Matt Gogel, who spent six years playing smaller tours from Asia to his native Kansas, captures his first PGA TOUR win at the 2002 AT&T Pebble Beach National Pro-Am.

Cinderella story,

Much has changed in the game since Arnold Palmer (left) took this shot at the
PGA Championship in 1971. However, he and Stephen Ames (above), during the
final round of the 2004 Cialis Western Open, display the same confidence
and concentration that characterizes PGA TOUR golf.

KELLY LUENG
is already giving back to her extended
community by volunteering at The First
Tee of Metropolitan New York, where
she learned the game.

# The First Tee

Kelly Leung is one of the hundreds of metropolitan New York-area kids who have taken advantage of the opportunities envisioned by the World Golf Foundation when it created The First Tee, with the support of the PGA TOUR, in November 1997. Its purpose is to provide golf access to those, especially children, who may not otherwise have the opportunity to play.

The First Tee experience provides learning facilities and educational programs throughout the country that use golf to promote character development and life-enhancing values. Constant throughout every aspect of the activities is The First Tee Life Skills Program. Used to explain and instill the inherent values of the game of golf, its instructors show participants how these values can transfer to other aspects of their lives. They are taught about responsibility, courtesy, how to make decisions by thinking about the possible consequences, how to set and define goals, the importance of maintaining a positive attitude, and showing respect for others.

Four days a week, Kelly leaves her home in Jamaica, Queens, and takes a bus and three trains to The First Tee experience at Mosholu Golf Course in the Bronx. The roundtrip journey takes almost four hours, but the destination is worth the effort.

Kelly, whose golf experience before joining The First Tee amounted to a few lessons at a driving range in Queens, knows that learning about core values is not the most exciting topic for teenagers. "Well, no one really wants to learn about that stuff," she says. "But after you hear about them so many times, learning what they mean and even being quizzed on them, you just kind of remember it and it sinks in. You do think about it outside of golf, like being responsible in situations, and you think 'Oh my God, I heard that in The First Tee.' It's repeated so much here that it almost becomes natural to think of it at school or at home."

For Kelly, the program has come full circle. She started with The First Tee as a freshman in high school after her mom found the program online. She spent the summer before her senior year at the Bronx High School of Science volunteering at The First Tee four times a week, then returned as the captain of her school's golf team. She's learned much more than just how to hit a ball. She's also learned the kind of life lessons that make a long commute, even by New York City standards, well worth the effort.

Kelly Leung is committed to The First Tee Experience.

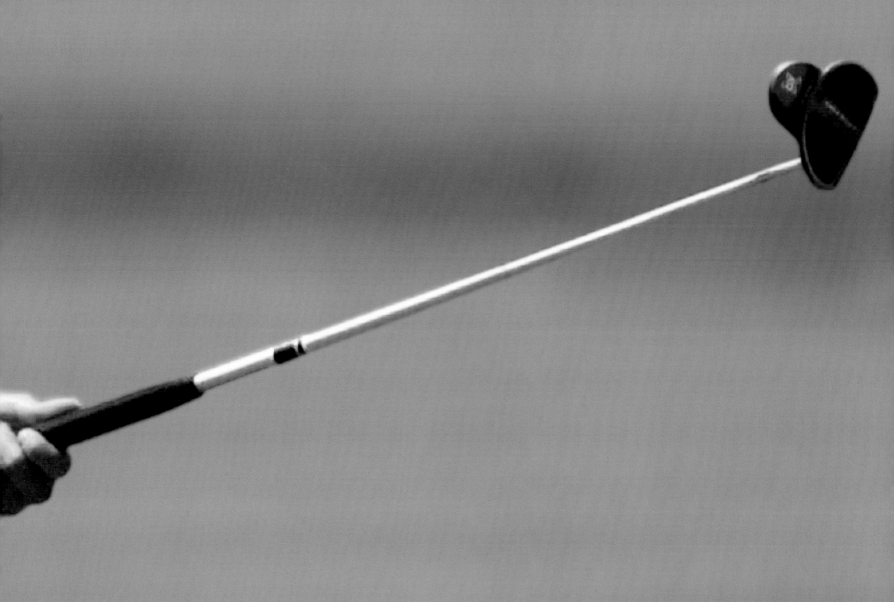

**SHIGEKI MARUYAMA**
reacts to the sight of a 39-foot,
par-saving putt disappearing into the
fifth hole at the Memorial Tournament.

THE TPC OF
SCOTTSDALE
is an oasis in the Sonoran Desert.
It is home of the FBR Open,
the largest spectator event on the
PGA TOUR, drawing galleries of
over half a million fans each year.

# a sense of place

by

DAVID BARRETT

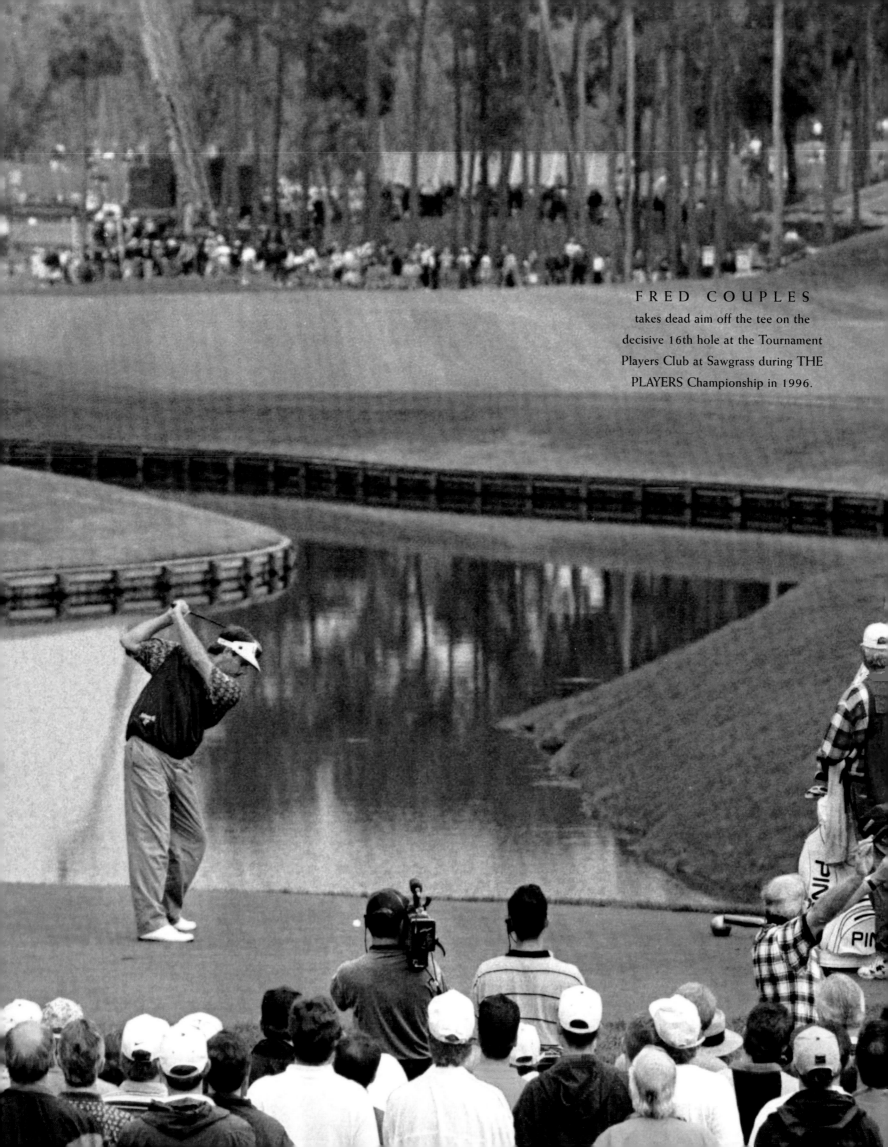

**FRED COUPLES** takes dead aim off the tee on the decisive 16th hole at the Tournament Players Club at Sawgrass during THE PLAYERS Championship in 1996.

Fred Couples stood in the 16th fairway at the Tournament Players Club at Sawgrass needing to make something happen if he was going to win THE PLAYERS Championship. Trailing Colin Montgomerie and Tommy Tolles by one, he was 220 yards from the hole, with a chance to reach the par 5 in two shots.

He knew he could get home with a 2-iron. But did he dare shoot at the flag and try to make an eagle? The right fringe of the 16th green ends abruptly with a wooden bulkhead and a drop-off to the water. From back in the fairway, the glittering pond to the right seems almost to swallow the much smaller green. It's an intimidating sight, designed not only to make the player consider his options but to test his mettle and resolve.

On Sunday, with the tournament on the line, it was also a test of his ability to execute under pressure. Couples decided to go for it. He planned a left-to-right shot. As it happened, he pushed it a bit, but not enough to find the water. Then he holed a dramatic twenty-five-foot eagle putt to grab the lead—emphatically.

A few minutes later, Montgomerie stood in the same 16th fairway, 230 yards from the hole. If he'd still led by one, he might have played it safe and laid up, or at least aimed for the left side of the green. Instead, down by one, he took his 3-wood and went for the heroic shot. He also planned a fade toward the flag, but his shot drifted too far right. Its splash dashed his hopes. Couples, who also birdied the 17th, would end up beating Montgomerie and Tolles by four strokes.

Such a stunning turnaround is just what the last three holes at the TPC at Sawgrass are designed to make possible. The 16th, 17th, and 18th, created by Pete Dye, make for exciting golf with any number of possible strategies and outcomes. The first two offer reasonable chances for birdies, but with water a prominent feature on all three holes, disaster lurks just around the corner.

# The last three holes at the TPC at Sawgrass make for exciting golf.

Couples won that 1996 PLAYERS Championship not by beating Montgomerie and Tolles head-to-head—they were playing in three different groups—but by handling the challenge of the closing stretch better than they did. The outcome demonstrated anew that the PGA TOUR player's real opponent is the field of play. Each golfer wages his own private battle against the golf course; the tournament standings are simply a compilation of those individual battles.

The fascinating and unique thing about golf is that the field of play, and thus the test for the players, varies so much from tournament to tournament. As the TOUR moves around the country, visiting some of the best and most challenging courses in the land, the players see varying terrain—hilly, flat, heavily wooded, nearly barren—and different kinds of grasses. The TOUR travels to courses with greens large and small, to courses with water hazards on nearly every hole and others where the only water is in the coolers. Conditions vary, too, with wind, the firmness of the greens, and the length of the rough changing from week to week.

It's as if baseball players found the distance between bases to be eighty-five feet in one ballpark and ninety-five feet in the next, or basketball players had to factor in the effect of the wind on their shots. That may be one reason there is such camaraderie among golfers—they are facing the same challenges, so they're all in it together.

"We play under a wide variety of conditions from week to week," says Jeff Sluman. "You have to figure it out real quick, or you're not going to last out here."

Jonathan Kaye reacts as his bunker shot onto the 13th barely misses the hole during the final round of the 2003 Buick Invitational at Torrey Pines in La Jolla, California.

Each golfer wages his own private battle against the golf course.

DAVID FROST
blasts a shot out of the water during
The Colonial at the Colonial Country
Club in Dallas, Texas, in 1998.

# BAY HILL
## CLUB & LODGE

in Orlando, Florida, is nestled among a
chain of lakes with plentiful mounds and
bunkers that require long, high
iron shots to hold its greens.

STEVE FLESCH found himself shoeless in a boulder-lined creek for his second shot on the fourth hole in the final round of the 2002 BellSouth Classic at the TPC at Sugarloaf in Duluth, Georgia.

The TOUR starts the year on the West Coast, playing on greens of Poa *annua* and bentgrass. The bermudagrass greens putt much differently in Florida where the much stronger grain must be accounted for. "You might have trouble with that for your first few years, especially if you didn't grow up on bermuda," says Mark O'Meara, another veteran.

Since each course offers its own challenges, players must start each week with a plan of how to attack that course. In a few exceptional cases, they might even start tweaking their games a couple of weeks before a tournament.

Scott McCarron used to practice hitting right-to-left shots with a 3-wood a couple of weeks before the Masters because that's a shot he needed at Augusta National. Now that the tees have been moved back, he finds he doesn't use that shot as much, but there is one drill he still finds very useful before he heads to Augusta.

"I start putting in my garage on the cement, where it's really fast," he says. "I'll try to hit putts just one inch on the cement. The greens are so fast at Augusta that there are some downhill putts where you're only trying to hit it one inch or two inches. That's tough to do unless you've practiced it."

## Each course offers its own challenges.

Aaron Baddeley hits an approach shot from the fairway toward the 18th green and a large crowd during the 2003 Nissan Open at the Riviera Country Club.

# Preparation can go out the window if conditions change.

Ernie Els hits out of a large bunker bordering the fairway on the sixth hole on a foggy day at the Pebble Beach Golf Links during the 100th U.S. Open in 2000.

The time to work on shots that might be required on a particular course is usually Tuesday and Wednesday of tournament week. When the greens are exceedingly soft, for example, players will try to take spin off their approach shots. If the ball has too much backspin, it will "dance" too much and the results will be unpredictable. It's better to hit a shot that will stop close to where it lands.

"In the AT&T Pebble Beach National Pro-Am, we often play in wet conditions. Instead of a sand wedge, you need to hit a 9-iron and take a half-swing," says Len Mattiace. "But we're not accustomed to hitting that shot, and if you haven't practiced it, it's hard to trust it."

Preparation is all well and good. But it can all go out the window if conditions change during a tournament. Mattiace remembers the 2000 PLAYERS Championship, when the greens were very firm on Sunday. "Then we had a rainstorm and had to come back and finish Monday morning. The greens had completely changed. We're grooved all week to putt a twenty-footer the same way, then all of a sudden the rain comes and it would be easy to leave it two feet short."

**HARBOUR TOWN**
boasts not only a beautiful setting on
Hilton Head Island in South Carolina,
but one of the PGA TOUR's most
familiar landmarks—the lighthouse that
provides a backdrop for the final hole.

LEN MATTIACE
had to perch precariously on the rim
of a lake to hit this shot on the third
hole during the first round of the
2003 Sony Open in Hawaii at Waialae
Country Club in Honolulu.

Often it goes the other way, particularly at major championships where the course setup walks the line between difficult and impossible. If there's no rain and the wind picks up on the weekend, the greens dry out and take on the characteristics of concrete. Just try landing and stopping a golf ball on your driveway, and you'll get an idea of what the players face.

"They are trying to get the golf courses right on the edge," says Sluman. "They might have the golf course dialed in the way they want, then a sudden spike in temperature or drop in humidity dries it out to the point where it gets scary out there. But it's just the business we're in."

In most cases it's not a matter of shooting at every flag or playing safe on every hole. The players' battle against the course is more like a fencing match, and the players need to know when to parry and when to thrust. With TOUR courses set up to extract a penalty for an aggressive shot that is just a little bit off, yet with sub-par scoring a necessity to post a good finish, it's a tricky proposition to know which holes to play for birdies and where to be content to shoot for pars.

"There is a time to look at risk/reward and be realistic with yourself," says O'Meara. "If I go for it, are the benefits minimal as opposed to the risk, or are they worth it?"

The players' battle against the course is more like a fencing match.

Phil Mickelson amidst a sea of bunkers on the eighth hole at the 2002 World Golf Championships-American Express Championship.

# You see what you're made of when you play a hole like that.

The island green on the 17th hole at the Tournament Players Club at Sawgrass offers a challenge as well as a stage to the golfer who can hit the green and then make his putt over the undulating surface.

Some holes make the player think as soon as he gets to the tee. An example of a hole offering a lot of options is the 393-yard, par-4 sixth at the Tournament Players Club at Sawgrass. "If you take a driver, you bring a very deep bunker on the left and trees on the right into play. But it's kind of nice to be able to hit a seventy-yard shot into the green," says Mattiace. "That gives you an advantage over the guy who hits a 3-iron off the tee and an 8-iron into the green. But only if you hit the fairway."

With today's players hitting the ball farther than ever due to improvements in equipment, physical training, and talent, TOUR courses have evolved along with them to continue to provide a thorough examination, both physically and mentally. New courses, including the TPC of Louisiana and the Rees Jones Course at Redstone in Houston, will measure more than 7,500 yards. Whether it's a 480-yard par-4 on one of the new layouts or the 137-yard par-3 island-green 17th at the TPC at Sawgrass, the idea is to give the players a formidable "opponent" in order to test their skills.

"When you play a hole like the 17th at Sawgrass, the stress is incredible," says Kenny Perry. "I like holes that put a little fear in you. You see what you're made of when you play a hole like that and, as a pro, that's what you're looking for."

JESPER PARNEVIK
must get creative with this shot from
among the trees along the third fairway
at the 2004 Sony Open in Hawaii at
Waialae Country Club.

PEBBLE BEACH boasts a marvelous combination of shotmaking and scenery, with the fourth through 10th holes lying along the edge of Carmel Bay.

# The Button Hole kids

Billy Andrade demonstrates his smooth golf swing as well as his dedication to young golfers during an instructional session for the Button Hole kids.

When the day's work is done, Ed Mauro often walks out of the office and down a path past the driving range to a point where he can get a good view of the golf facility that he first dreamed of building in his hometown of Providence, Rhode Island, less than a decade ago. He sees grandmothers sitting and watching their grandchildren knock balls around the Button Hole Short Course and Teaching Center. He sees the future of America ethnically, with many races walking on the green grass, clubs in hand. It's a good feeling.

Brad Faxon knows just how he feels. "I like to come up here and just sit and watch. Some of these kids live in really tough situations. They come up here, and you show them how to hold a golf club, how to swing it, and then they hole a few putts and they start to have fun. They start to enjoy themselves, and you do, too."

As the driving force behind the facility, Mauro knew that the involvement of two fellow Rhode Island natives—Faxon, a resident of Barrington, and Billy Andrade, who grew up in Bristol—would be critical to the program's success.

While both have traveled the world during their PGA TOUR careers, their Rhode Island roots remain strong. The mere mention of their involvement with Button Hole led to a $50,000 donation from a local bank. Their help, along with that of countless other volunteers, led a fundraising campaign that turned a former gravel pit near downtown Providence into a premier youth facility. Today the formerly crime-ridden site offers nine holes ranging from 65 to 140 yards, a 25-bay lighted, double-ended driving range, and a place where young people learn a lot about themselves.

Despite a hectic TOUR schedule, Andrade and Faxon make their presence felt at the facility as often as possible, highlighted by Faxon's annual youth clinic, which drew 459 kids in 2004. After hitting balls in front of a huge audience, Faxon signed hats and talked to almost each one of the kids in attendance. In past years, he has stayed on afterward to play nine holes with the volunteers. Andrade often shows up unannounced throughout the year to work with whomever is there on any particular day.

Here the game of golf, and with it the lessons of honesty, humility, and perseverance are being taught to inner-city kids who had never given the game a second thought.

But spending time with the Button Hole kids is not the only charitable work by the duo, who have won 11 events between them on the PGA TOUR. For years Faxon and Andrade have run their own Charities for Children fund, and each summer they also organize and participate in the star-studded CVS Charity Classic, an event that raised over $1 million in 2004.

"These guys are givers," Mauro says of Faxon and Andrade, who serve as honorary co-chairmen of Button Hole. "I don't call them too often, but when I do, they are there for us. That's the way these guys are."

**BRAD FAXON**

drives from the fourth tee at
the AT&T Pebble Beach National
Pro-Am at the Spyglass Hill Golf
Course in Pebble Beach in 2003.

The fairway lies ahead in scattered carpets of green from the 16th tee
at the 2003 Phoenix Open at the TPC at Scottsdale (above). PGA West at
La Quinta, California (left), plays host to the Bob Hope Chrysler Classic,
where David Duval once shot his 59 in the final round.

# The Monster is back

Craig Parry celebrates his eagle from the fairway that defeated Scott Verplank at Doral's infamous 18th hole in 2004.

The Monster is back. The par-4 18th hole at Doral's Blue Course regained its status as the toughest hole on the PGA TOUR in 2004 thanks to a new tee that added twenty-four yards, making it play at 467. Now, Doral's 18th leads a pack of backbreaking holes that test the skills of the world's best players to the utmost.

How could a difference of twenty-four yards make a hole so much tougher? The answer suggests some of the factors that the pros find most vexing. In the case of No. 18 at Doral, the added length affected the landing area for tee shots. In recent years, players had been carrying their tee shots to the widest part of the fairway, past the point where the pond on the left of the hole juts into it. With the tee moved back, the players are forced to steer their tee shots into a narrow area between the water on the left and bunkers on the right, just as in the old days. And with more water on the left for the approach, the second shot also becomes more dangerous with a longer club.

So it's all the more impressive that Craig Parry chose the 18th at Doral to hit the most spectacular shot seen in many years, holing a 6-iron from 176 yards for an eagle to win a sudden-death playoff over Scott Verplank. He did it on a hole that played to a 4.48 stroke average in 2004.

But Doral's 18th is far from the only hole on the TOUR where bogeys are almost as common as pars. Quail Hollow's 18th is 478 yards, par-4, and plays to an average of 4.42. This hole is long, the second shot is uphill, a creek guards the left side on both the drive and approach, and there are trees and bunkers to the right. Oh yes, the green is undulating, too. David Toms finished with a quadruple bogey eight in 2003—fortunately, he came to the hole with an eight-stroke lead.

The 12th at Torrey Pines is a 477-yard par-4 that averages out at 4.39 on the TOUR. There's plenty of length on this tree-lined hole that heads straight for the ocean and often plays into the wind, but it could play even harder. There's a tee farther back at 504 yards that the TOUR doesn't use.

Firestone's 16th, at 667 yards, is a par-5 that averages 5.39. A three-shot par-5 where the third shot is a treacherous one over a pond—with more than a wedge if the player finds trouble from the tee. This is another monster restored to its former glory, with a new back tee adding 42 yards in 2003.

Bay Hill's 17th is a par-3, 219 yards. Average: 3.31. Water is in play on the front and right and the bunkers on the left and back. But the thing that makes it the toughest par-3 on TOUR is the firmness of the green, making the relatively shallow putting surface tough to hold with a long iron.

ERNIE ELS
hits a chip shot to the
18th green while fans watch
from beyond the water during
the 1999 Doral-Ryder Open.

NEMACOLIN
WOODLANDS
is nestled in the bucolic Pennsylvania
countryside. It is poised to display
its fall colors around the fourth hole
during the final round of the
84 LUMBER Classic in 2004.

"I love links golf.
I like to be able to
start the ball way out
to the left and
in there, or run it up, or throw
it up on top and spin it."

TIGER WOODS

Tiger Woods twists his body and his swing to cut the ball
around an obstacle in a difficult shot.

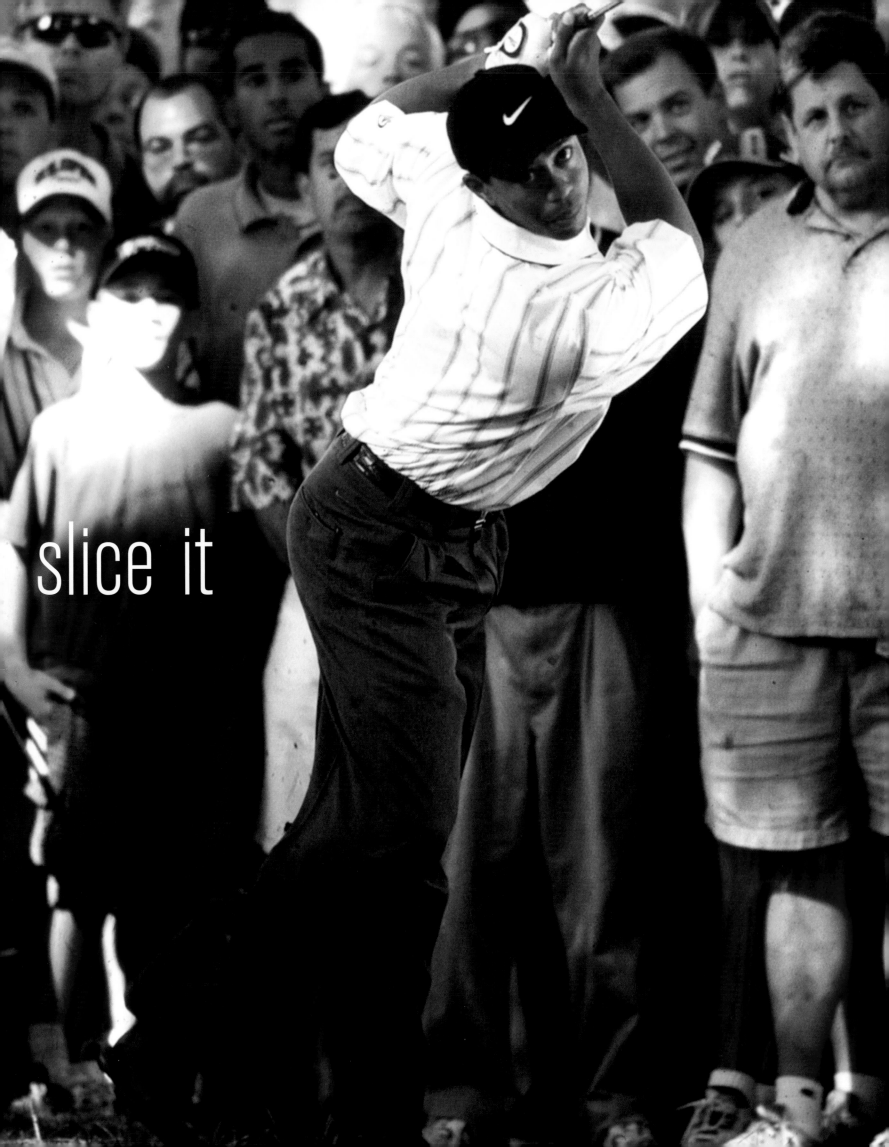

slice it

**ROBERT ALLENBY**

plays from a shallow greenside bunker
on the second hole during his match in
foursomes at The Presidents Cup in 2003
at The Links Fancourt Golf Course,
George, South Africa.

# The legacy of the lambs

The original designers of golf's sand bunkers were not architects, nor even human. They were sheep. Today, the legacy of the lambs makes for one of the most critical elements in the design of PGA TOUR courses.

Sand bunkers evolved naturally on the early Scottish links. Sheep would gather behind any small rise on the mostly flat land to shelter from the wind. Eventually, they would create a hole, which would collect blown sand. Presto! The golf courses became dotted with bunkers.

In the late 19th century, the idea of designing golf courses took hold. In a clear case of art imitating nature, digging strategically-placed bunkers became part of building a course.

Today, bunkers come in all shapes, sizes, and depths. The original "pot" bunkers of Scotland—small, deep pits—are the most difficult to escape. Often, advancing the ball toward the hole from a pot bunker is impossible, and the unfortunate player must hit out sideways or even backwards.

Bunkers are more likely to be strategic than penal in the United States. The placement of fairway bunkers, in particular, often gives players options off the tee. If bunkers pinch the fairway, for example, players might choose to lay up short of them. Or, bunkers might be placed in such a way as to give long hitters the option of trying to carry the ball over them.

Greenside bunkers, of course, have always been a staple of golf architecture. But TOUR players have become so adept out of the sand that the fear factor is gone. In 2003, they got up and down from greenside bunkers 49.6 percent of the time, and you'll often hear a player yell for an errant shot to "get in the bunker!" instead of what might be a more difficult lie in the rough.

Still, there are unfriendly bunkers on the PGA TOUR. One of the strangest is at the par-3 sixth at Riviera Country Club, site of the Nissan Open, where architect George Thomas put a bunker in the middle of the green, a gambit that no architect would dare today. Somehow, it works. One of the TOUR's greediest bunkers is at the front left of the 16th green at Castle Pines Golf Club, site of The International, referred to as a "collection" bunker because any shot landing on the left front of the green diabolically feeds down into it. One of the largest is at the 11th at the Tournament Players Club at Sawgrass, extending the last one hundred yards of the hole and wrapping around the green, so far below the putting surface that ladders are placed to help the players get out.

The size of the bunker raises the prospect of the sand shot that regularly causes a tightening in the throat of even a TOUR player—the long explosion. Picking shots out of fairway bunkers is something any TOUR pro can do. So is the routine greenside bunker shot. But an explosion that must carry forty or fifty yards, then stop on a slick green, is a shot that requires both power and delicacy. It's the one shot that makes professionals remember how stepping into the sand feels to amateurs.

Charles Howell III explodes his ball from the bunker on the 11th hole in the final round of the HP Classic at English Turn Golf and Country Club in New Orleans, Louisiana.

**TORREY PINES**
is one of the toughest venues
on the PGA TOUR. Located in
La Jolla, California, prevailing
ocean breezes play havoc,
especially at the 12th hole.

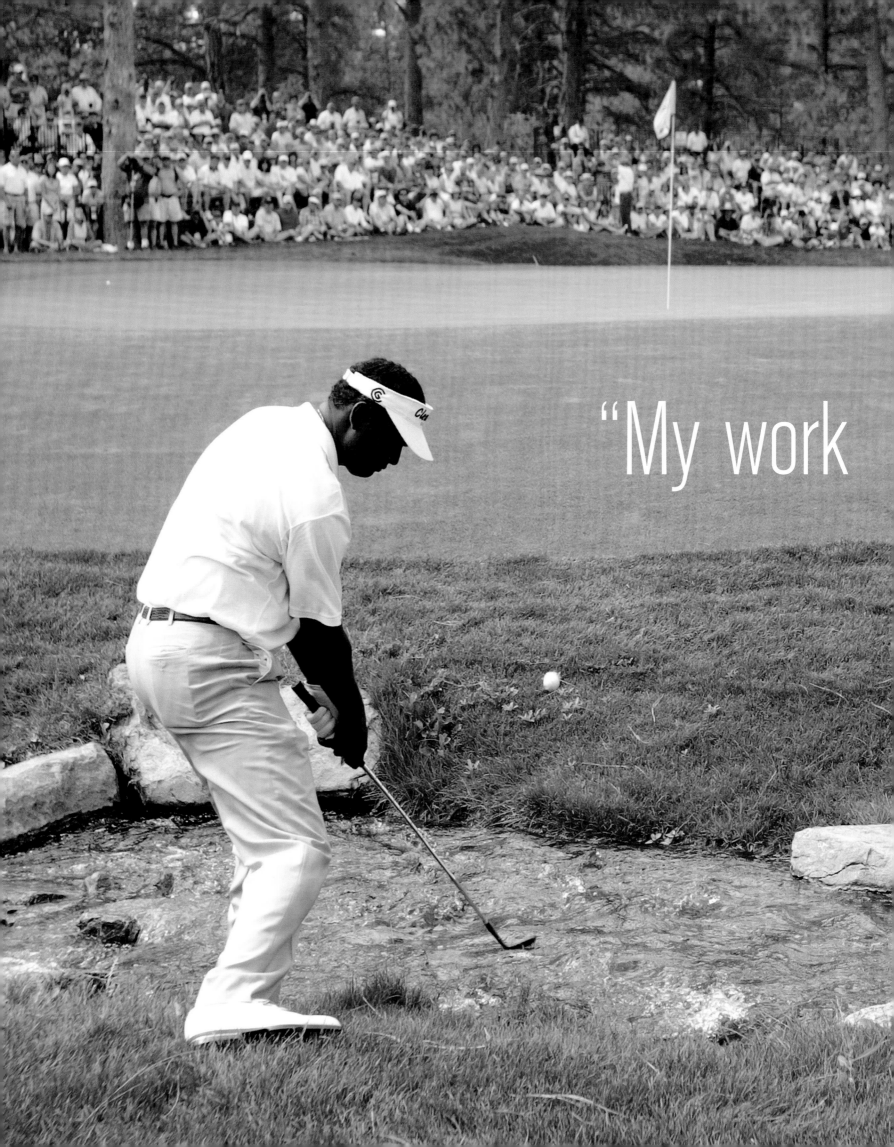

"My work

is something I really love.
So is it really work?"

VIJAY SINGH

Vijay Singh chips across a fast-running creek onto the 14th green
during the 2003 INTERNATIONAL at Castle Pines Golf Club.

# The Sunday pin

Stewart Cink winces as his birdie putt stops short of the hole at the edge of the green during the final round at the 2004 Buick Invitational.

Compared to an average golf course, a course set up for a PGA TOUR event is like a Grand Prix racetrack contrasted with the streets in your neighborhood. If you're just used to driving the family sedan, you'd better watch out in the corners, because crashes are likely.

While a 5-handicapper might see a pro shooting a 72 and figure, "I could do that on a good day," the truth is it's a different game out there. The rough is higher. Fairways and greens are firmer. But the biggest difference is the hole locations. They're not all close to the middle of the green. If you're going to make pars and birdies on the PGA TOUR, you're going to have to find your way to some pins that are tucked just a few steps away from big trouble.

In the last couple of years, it's gotten even more perilous. With players hitting so many wedges and short irons into the greens thanks to the current power game, the TOUR field staff has changed the minimum distance from the hole to the edge of the PGA TOUR green to a mere sliver of three yards. "When you look at it from the fairway, sometimes it looks like the pin isn't on the green," says Kenny Perry.

"We go to three paces only when we know they're hitting a short iron," says Mike Shea, the TOUR's senior director of rules. "You'll never see it that close on a 4-iron shot."

Still, you could put the flag two inches from the edge and many TOUR players would aim right at it when they have a wedge in their hands.

The common perception is that the TOUR saves the hardest hole locations for the final round on Sunday. That's not quite true, because the TOUR tries for a balanced mix every day—some holes front and some back; some holes left and some right. But Shea says he does use as many of what he calls "ace locations" for the final round as he can.

"What we're trying to do is make the player think," says Shea. "When you put the hole location close to a lateral hazard or deep bunker, you really challenge the player from a mental standpoint. If he misses on the wrong side of the hole, he's left with a difficult or impossible up and down. Now he's got to consider hitting the ball fifteen to twenty feet from the hole towards the center of the green and trying to make a birdie putt from there."

An example of a "Sunday pin" is the 17th hole at the Tournament Players Club at Sawgrass, where in the final round the hole is always located in a small bowl on the right of the green toward the back, just four steps away from the water. The safe shot to the center of the green leaves a tricky long putt over a ridge. To have a realistic shot at a birdie, the player needs to challenge the water to the right and behind the hole—if he dares. Welcome to the racetrack.

GREG NORMAN
blasts a shot from a steep bunker
to a close pin placement after
digging in to steady himself
during the 2001 Skins Game
at the Landmark Golf Club
in Indio, California.

Craig Stadler (above) shoots his way out of the Church Pews at the U.S. Open
in Oakmont, Pennsylvania, a bunker that sometimes requires a golfer to
give ground in order to escape. Davis Love III (right) hacks his way
out of the wicked rough at Pebble Beach.

# Man against the hole

When Charles Howell III stepped to the 10th tee at Riviera Country Club on the second hole of a playoff against Mike Weir at the 2003 Nissan Open, the golf hole became as important in the drama as the players. Riviera's 10th exemplifies the distinctive holes on the TOUR that force players to make delicate judgments and hit precise shots, holes that impose consequences for mistakes.

Howell's decision was to try to make something happen. He hit his driver on the 310-yard par-4, with the idea of reaching the putting surface and giving himself a putt for an eagle. His shot sailed to the right, though, leaving him a nightmarishly long bunker shot. By being aggressive, he brought bogey into the picture—and the end of the tournament.

Weir laid up off the tee with an iron and hit a 74-yard wedge second shot to nine feet. Advantage Weir. Howell responded by hitting his nearly impossible bunker shot to five feet. Advantage Howell. Then Weir made his birdie putt. Howell didn't. Game, set, and match to Weir. Two ways to play the hole and a wide variety of possible outcomes for each. That's one of the characteristics that make certain holes fan favorites.

The par-5 16th hole at the Tournament Players Club at Sawgrass is 507 yards. It's reachable in two shots, but the green juts into a pond along the right side, and the hole is sometimes cut within twenty feet of the water. A large tree on the left side creates trouble for those who would opt to play safe and lay up, but two good shots are rewarded with an eagle chance. "If you're playing well and execute correctly, you feel like it wasn't that hard," says Jeff Sluman. "The next day you try it, and you make double bogey."

At Muirfield Village, the 14th hole is a 363-yard par-4. A creek crosses the fairway some 250 yards from the tee, forcing most players to lay up. The excitement comes with the second shot, with the creek guarding the right side of a narrow sliver of a green that slopes precipitously toward the water. A good wedge shot sets up a birdie putt, but a player who misses the green in the large bunker to the left isn't thinking about a par. He's just hoping to keep his third shot on the green.

Like Riviera's 10th, the 296-yard 15th hole at the Tournament Players Club at River Highlands is a driveable par-4 that can be even more influential in the tournament because it comes later in the round. Some players can reach the green with a 3-wood, but with water to the left it's a dangerous shot. A tee shot on or near the green sets up an easy birdie, but the hole extracts a toll for errant shots—there are generally about three times as many double bogeys (and worse) as there are eagles.

Mike Weir hits his second shot on the 18th hole of the final round of the 2003 Nissan Open. He won the tournament in a playoff with Charles Howell III.

PHIL MICKELSON
drives down the fairway between rows
of palm and eucalyptus trees at the
Bob Hope Chrysler Classic at
La Quinta, California, in 2002.

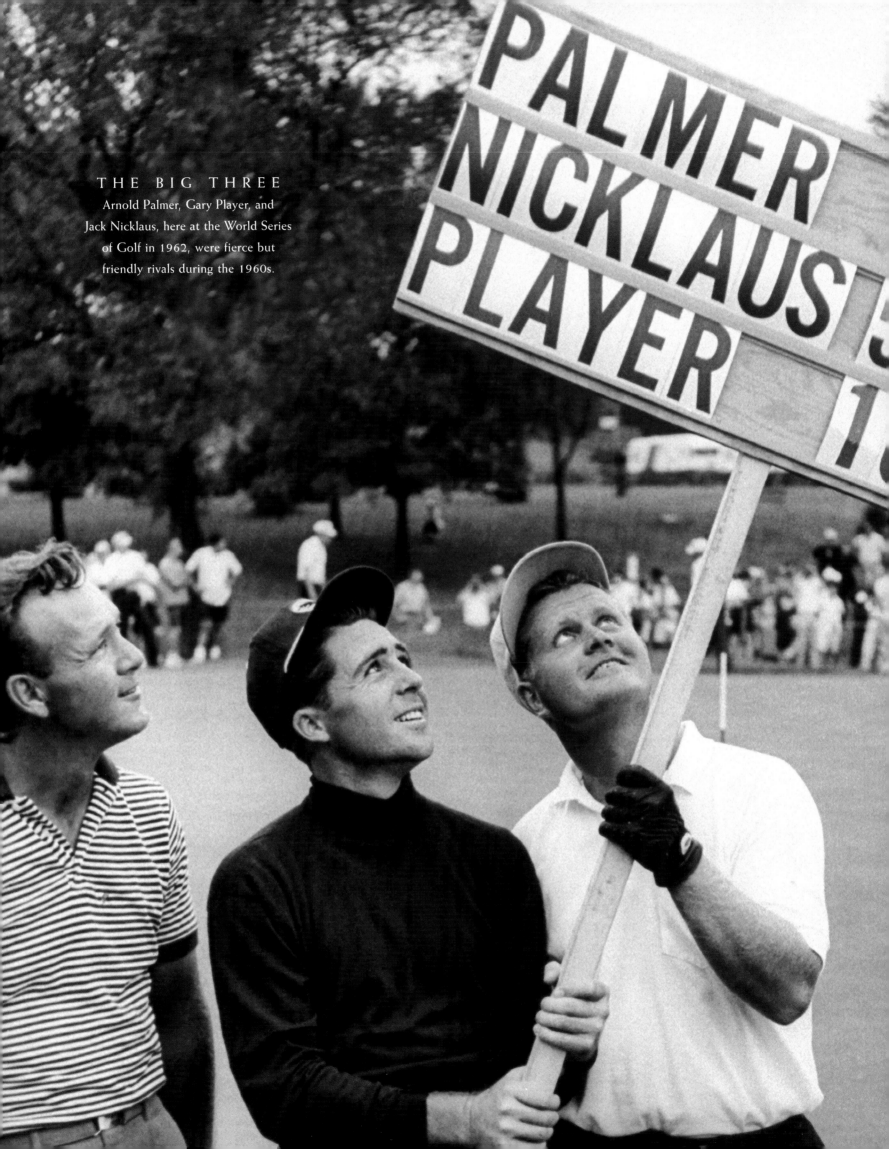

## THE BIG THREE
Arnold Palmer, Gary Player, and
Jack Nicklaus, here at the World Series
of Golf in 1962, were fierce but
friendly rivals during the 1960s.

# the legacy of greatness

by

BOB CULLEN

**BILL HAAS**
made his PGA TOUR professional debut in June 2004 after earning honors as the top college player in the country.

During the 2004 Booz Allen Classic, a young man named Bill Haas stepped onto the 10th tee to make his professional debut. He looked professional, with sharply creased, iron-gray slacks and a peach-colored shirt. He chatted for a moment with the young woman who surveys the equipment the pros are using. When he was introduced, he tipped his cap to scattered applause. Then he pulled out a 2-iron, took a couple of practice swings, and striped a shot that rose quickly against the blue sky, drew slightly, and bounced to rest 250 yards out on the proper side of the fairway to approach the green.

It was a good start for a twenty-two-year-old rookie, but it was not surprising. Three generations of Bill Haas's family have played on the PGA TOUR. His great-uncle, Bob Goalby, won the 1968 Masters and accumulated eleven victories on the TOUR. His father, Jay Haas, played on the TOUR for twenty-eight years and in 2004, at fifty, became the second oldest player ever to play on the Ryder Cup team. Jay's younger brother, Jerry, played the TOUR in the 1990s. So it was understandable that Bill Haas should make his debut knowing how to dress, how to acknowledge the gallery, how to select a club on a short par 4, and how to hit it. It was predictable that he would play golf well and honor the game. The legacy of thousands of pros who have made the TOUR is, for him, a personal legacy.

## It's a standard of excellence, a standard of conduct, a respect for the game.

Bill Haas's great-uncle, Bob Goalby, tees off in the 1973 Masters with Sam Snead (left) and Doug Ford.

# That legacy has been built over more than a century.

Jerry Haas, Bill's uncle and Jay's brother, coached Bill at Wake Forest after his own days on the PGA TOUR.

When he thinks of what he learned from his father and his great-uncle, Bill Haas does not immediately talk about his golf swing, though he has a very good one. "I think the way my dad's handled himself is something that a lot of people respect," he says. "At the U.S. Open last year, someone said, 'Jay Haas, one of the greatest guys on TOUR,' and then I think it was ESPN's Chris Berman who said, 'One of the greatest guys ever.' That means more to my dad than anything anyone's ever said about his golf game."

His father passed along those standards mostly by example. But Bill Haas remembers a moment when the teaching was more direct. The Haas family lived at the time near the sixth hole at Thornblade Country Club in Greenville, South Carolina. "I was a high school freshman, I guess, and my dad and I were playing No. 7. I hit a bad chip and I got mad and took a big swing at the dirt. The grass went onto the green—a really bad act on my part. And he just said, 'Go in. I'll deal with you when I get done.' He made me walk into my house and I had to sit there till he finished eighteen holes."

Thus was the time-tested legacy of the PGA TOUR passed along from father to son. It's a standard of excellence in golf, of course. But it's more than that. It's a standard of conduct, a respect for the game. That legacy has been built over more than a century.

JAY HAAS
in action at the 2004
Buick Invitational, is a nine-time
winner on the PGA TOUR.

WALTER HAGEN
is closely watched as he lines
up a shot in a match between
English and American pros.

It's difficult to pinpoint the date on which the idea of an organized golf tour was born. The first U.S. Open championship was played in 1895 at the Newport Golf and Country Club in Rhode Island, and won by twenty-one-year-old Horace Rawlins. His prize was $150. The same year, members of the St. Andrews Club in Yonkers, New York, the first permanent American golf club, invited Scottish pro Willie Park Jr., a two-time British Open winner, to come to the United States and give some exhibitions.

Five years after that, in 1900, sporting goods manufacturer A. G. Spalding marketed a new gutta-percha golf ball called the Vardon Flyer. The company invited the ball's namesake, the great English player Harry Vardon, to spend the better part of the year touring the United States, giving exhibitions. That may have been the first instance of an equipment company sponsoring a professional golfer in this country, though Vardon did not wear a cap or other clothing with the word "Spalding" printed on the front. It was also the first instance of a professional golf "tour" in the United States, though Vardon played almost exclusively in exhibitions rather than tournaments. (He did take time to win the U.S. Open.)

The true genesis of a competitive tour may have been young Walter Hagen's triumph at the U.S. Open in 1914. Hagen was just the third "home-bred" player to win the national championship. More important, Hagen was the first showman. With his pomaded hair, his luxurious clothes, and his clutch game, he was the sort of athlete Americans would pay to see in the era of Babe Ruth and Jack Dempsey.

After Hagen arrived on the scene, the concept of an annual golf tour began to evolve more rapidly, growing over several decades from a series of exhibitions interspersed with the occasional tournament to a winter tour in Florida and California, then to a ten-month circuit by the late 1940s.

# It's difficult to pinpoint when the idea of an organized golf tour was born.

ARNOLD PALMER
is in a familiar setting amid
the pines at Augusta National
in April 2004.

The first generations of touring professionals were, almost exclusively, ex-caddies. As one of the best of them, Gene Sarazen, once noted, "The people we caddied for in those days were very high-class people." From the outset, touring professionals strove to prove that they belonged in that company.

It was not that they didn't have rough edges. One early professional named Lefty Stackhouse was reported to have gotten so mad at his putter that he tied it to the rear bumper of his car and dragged it to the next tournament as punishment. Some of the players drank, some of them cussed, and some of them chased women. But there was always an overriding code that has its echoes in the thing Bill Haas learned from his father: respect for the game. It was passed along largely by example.

Tommy Bolt, who began touring in the 1940s, remembers the first touring professional he ever saw—a man named Al Espinosa, who came one day to the club in Shreveport, Louisiana, where Bolt was a caddie. Bolt was so poor that he sometimes slept in bunkers at the course. When he saw Espinosa's buttery plus fours and two-tone shoes, he was transfixed. Bolt vowed then and there that he was going to be a touring professional. "All I had," he recalled recently, "was two pair of khaki pants, and I didn't want to ever wear khaki again." In all his years as a touring pro, he never did.

There was always an overriding code: respect for the game.

Like most touring professionals at the time, Gene Sarazen (left) and Walter Hagen (center) learned the game as caddies before they went pro.

**TOMMY BOLT**
salutes the gallery at the
1958 U.S. Open, which he won.
Bolt recorded 15 professional
victories and is enshrined in
the World Golf Hall of Fame.

JOHNNY MILLER
won the U.S. Open in 1973
and 24 other PGA TOUR
events in his career.

Fewer TOUR players these days start out as caddies, and none of them sleeps in a bunker. But the best traditions of the game are still passed along, largely by example, as one golf generation's legacy to the next. Golf, unlike any other sport, presents opportunities for the greats of the past to mingle with the best players of the present—and to teach them.

Davis Love III recounted one such event in his memoir, *Every Shot I Take*. He was selected for The Presidents Cup in 1996, and his captain was Arnold Palmer. Love recalled how Palmer spoke one night to the American team at dinner. "He said it was our responsibility to make sure the young players coming up now learned from us just as we learned from the veterans when we were joining the TOUR.  He said it was critical to respect the traditions of the game. He said our biggest responsibility was to those who love the game: we need to be generous with our time and energy to the game's true fans."

The greats of the past mingle with the best players of the present—and teach them.

Arnold Palmer and Davis Love III, who competed as captain and player on the 1996 United States Presidents Cup team, come from different generations but share their commitment to the game.

# If these young players keep their eyes open, they will learn a lot about their profession.

Teaching permeates the TOUR, building on golf's unique ability to span generations. There are practice rounds matching older players with younger ones at major championships like the Masters. The three TOUR events hosted each year by Palmer (the Bay Hill Invitational), Jack Nicklaus (the Memorial Tournament), and Byron Nelson (the EDS Byron Nelson Championship) give newer generations a chance to see the way the greats of the past handle themselves. A seamless web is woven. Hagen played with Sarazen, who played with Bolt and Hogan and Nelson, who played with Palmer and Nicklaus, who play today with Woods, Mickelson, Singh, and Els.

Mickelson loved the way Palmer treated the fans and volunteers at the U.S. Open of 1994, Palmer's last as a player. Mickelson recalls how Palmer spent an hour and a half signing autographs in the volunteer tent. "You guys spent hours on end helping out with this event," he said, "helping it run smoothly, and yet you don't have a chance to go out and see any golf at all. I wanted to come here and let you know how much we appreciate it." Palmer signed autographs for roughly 1,000 people.

"I thought that was what professional golf should be, the way professionals should handle themselves," Mickelson says. "The person I've tried to emulate the most is Arnold Palmer."

Thus the torch is passed, from Palmer to Mickelson, from Jay Haas to Bill Haas. No doubt, decades from now, young professionals as yet unborn will be teeing it up on occasion with players like Love, Mickelson, and, if he is both lucky and good, Bill Haas. If these young players keep their eyes open, they will learn a lot about their profession. They may not even be aware that they're learning from the likes of Hagen, Sarazen, Nelson, Palmer, and Nicklaus. But they will be.

**BYRON NELSON**
won eleven consecutive
tournaments in 1945 and set
a lasting example with his sense
of humor and his generosity.

**JACK NICKLAUS**
watches his putt roll toward the hole
during the 1965 Thunderbird Open.

# Tuesdays with Mr. Nicklaus

He cannot remember when he played his first practice round with Jack Nicklaus, but Glen Day remembers very well the things he's learned from the man he refers to only as "Mr. Nicklaus."

"I guess I started playing practice rounds with Gary (Jack Nicklaus's son) when we were both playing in Europe. Then when his dad showed up there for a tournament, I'd play with him. I was surprised that Mr. Nicklaus was so approachable. He's a nice gentleman and a nice man."

Thus began one of those relationships that passes on the values of one generation to the next. Nicklaus still played a partial schedule on the PGA TOUR, and that meant he needed partners for his practice rounds. Based on that, a friendship grew between a man with 73 career victories and a man with one.

"I might call him up and find out when he was playing in a tournament, or he might call and say, 'Hey, when are we playing on Tuesday?'" says Day. "I guess you could say he was my favorite player when I was growing up, but I treat Mr. Nicklaus the same way I treat Gary. He might give me a hard time, and I might give him a hard time."

The mentoring between Nicklaus and Day was partly about golf. "He's never taken my arm and said, 'Glen, you ought to be doing it this way.' He might say, 'I think you need to look at this; here's another option, a strategy option.' Or I might ask him a question and he's more than happy to help with a swing tip or putting or chipping or how a green is going to play. The first year I played the Masters I went and got the yardage book. When I was in Florida, I went to his house and gave him the book and said, 'Please tell me how to play this golf course.' And he went through every hole, saying, 'Well, I've always hit it there, and if you hit it here, the ball does this and if you hit it there, the ball does that.' He didn't have to do that."

He got a still stronger sense of the Nicklaus family ethos from Barbara Nicklaus, Jack's wife. Some years ago, Day and his wife, Jennifer, had just moved into a condominium in South Florida when Jennifer felt she might be having a miscarriage. Desperate, Day dialed the Nicklaus's number and asked where the nearest hospital was. Jack gave him directions. "It wasn't five minutes after we got to the emergency room that Barbara Nicklaus showed up. She said, 'Jennifer, you sit down.' Then she went in and said, 'I'm Barbara Nicklaus and we need to see Dr. Such-and-such and Dr. Such-and-such and we need to get this done and that done.' We didn't ask her to come down and do that. It just shows you how great the lady is and how nice the family is."

When he thinks about it, Glen Day says the legacy he picked up from those Tuesdays with Mr. Nicklaus is class. "That's what he has—class."

Glen Day won the MCI Classic-Heritage of Golf in 1999 for his only TOUR victory.

# "Listen, I just saw the I have ever seen...some fellow from Virginia by the name of Sam Snead."

GENE SARAZEN

Sam Snead, thought by many to have the most fluid, powerful swing in golf,
learned by hitting with a club he fashioned from an old buggy whip.

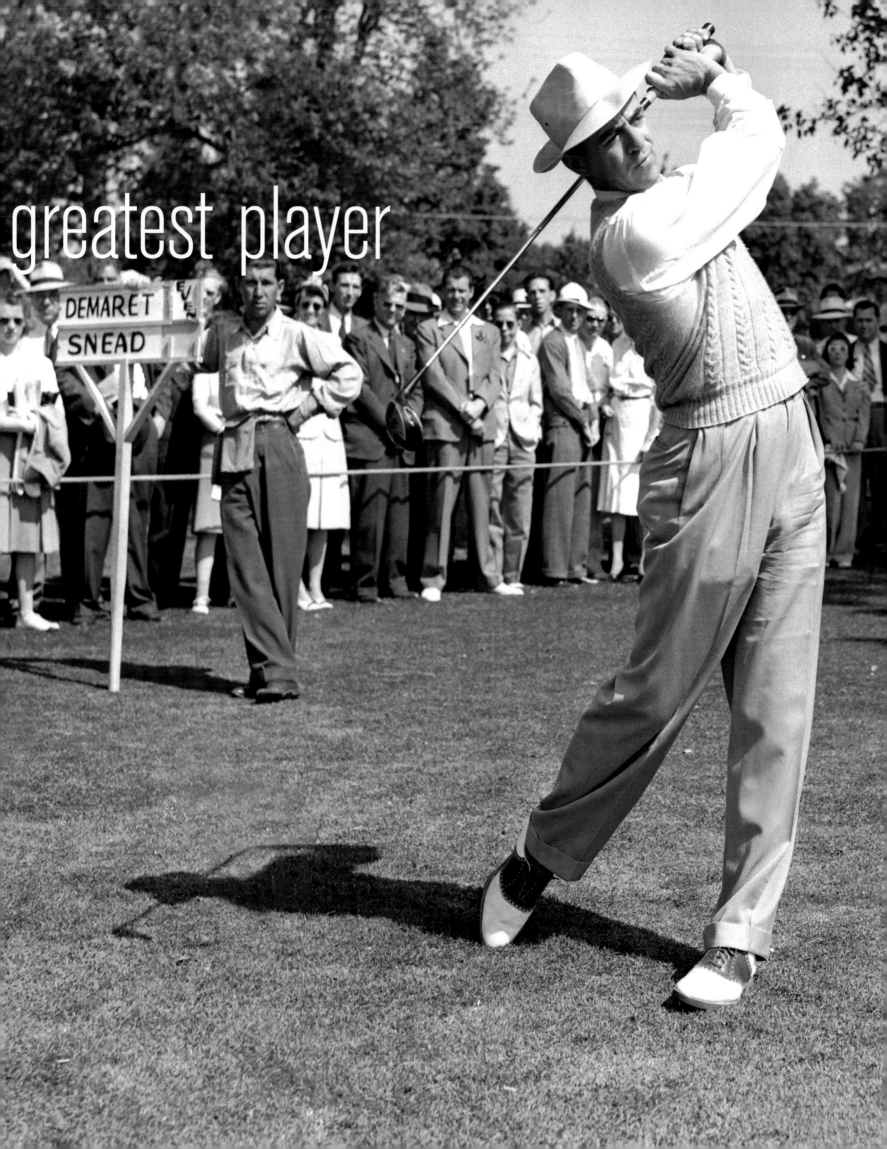

greatest player

KENNY PERRY
reacts to his tee shot on the
eighth hole at THE PLAYERS
Championship at the Tournament
Players Club at Sawgrass in 2004.

# Lessons for life

If you take Interstate 65 north from Nashville, up over the Kentucky border to the town of Franklin, you'll find a course called Country Creek. It belongs to Kenny Perry, who's been on the TOUR since 1987.

Pretty much anybody can play at Country Creek, which is by design. Perry built it with wide fairways, few bunkers, and lots of room on the right side of every hole, where the hackers hit it. Country Creek is not only playable, it's affordable. It costs $28 to play, with a cart.

A lot of those who take advantage of it are kids. "We pretty much give kids access to the facility, if they're promising and I feel like they're not just goofing around," says the owner.

Perry built the course in the mid-1990s, using his TOUR earnings and a loan. He bought up three farms, laid out the holes, and with friends and relatives, did a lot of the labor. He did it because when he was growing up in Franklin, his family could afford to belong to the only course in town, which had nine holes and was private. A lot of his friends could not.

Perry hated to see anyone from his town have to drive 30 miles away just to play golf. "So my brother-in-law, Bobby Bush, and I came up with the idea to build it and give something to the town."

Country Creek is the home course for the boys' and girls' golf teams at the local high school, Franklin-Simpson. Every spring, Perry takes six weeks off from the TOUR to serve as assistant coach. "I've got a system where I bring out my laptop and set up cameras front and back and I can split-screen them and definitely show them what's wrong with their golf swing. I can teach them a lot about golf, which is pretty important at that age," the assistant coach says.

Perry teaches more than the mechanics of the golf swing at Country Creek. "I teach them that it's a game you can't control, a game that probably will beat you every day you go out. It humbles you, it teaches you patience, and it will keep you out of trouble. I get pretty serious with them, and they don't want to go out and party. They're out at the range every day." Perry says golf is "a lot like life," and coming from him, the words sound original.

Country Creek hosts about 30,000 rounds of golf a year. It employs about 25 people, including some kids on a co-op program from the high school. Three of the golf team alumni, including Kenny's son Justin, have earned collegiate golf scholarships. "I think that's pretty neat," says Kenny Perry. So is the whole operation.

Perry won the Memorial Tournament in 2003.

Four of the game's greats (above) prepare to tee off. From left, Gene Sarazen, Bobby Jones,
Walter Hagen, and Tommy Armour. Jones, though he remained an amateur
throughout his competitive career, loved playing with the pros.
Chi Chi Rodriguez (left), at the 1964 U.S. Open, came out of the caddie yards of
Puerto Rico to win eight times on the PGA TOUR and 22 times on the Champions Tour
and earn World Golf Hall of Fame recognition.

JACK NICKLAUS

plays from the rough as he wins
his fourth U.S. Open at Baltusrol
in 1980.

# The World Golf Hall of Fame

The World Golf Hall of Fame outside St. Augustine, Florida, covers the history of golf.

There is a place where golf's legacy lives, where the game's traditions and legends are tangible and on display. It's the World Golf Hall of Fame in St. Augustine, Florida.

The Hall has everything from Sam Snead's childhood lunch box to the shirt Annika Sorenstam wore when she teed it up at the Bank of America Colonial in 2003. More important, it honors the game's finest players, along with teachers, administrators, and architects whose contributions have bettered the game. It's one of the most powerful ways that golf has devised to transmit its traditions and standards from one generation to the next, and it inspires awe even in its members.

As Ben Crenshaw said at his induction in 2002, "There are so many people here I revere. History and tradition are what this game is about. I can't believe I'm part of it."

The Hall, established in St. Augustine in 1998, is supported by the PGA TOUR and 25 other golf governing bodies from around the world. There are five avenues for induction: a PGA TOUR/Champions Tour ballot, the LPGA point system, an international ballot, a lifetime achievement category, and a veteran's category. Though the criteria differ in the categories for great players, all of them require a significant number of TOUR victories and major championships. The lifetime achievement category honors individuals who have supported the game primarily outside the ropes of tournament play. The veteran's category is for players whose major achievements occurred before 1974, when the forerunner of the current Hall was founded by the PGA of America in Pinehurst, North Carolina.

There are over 100 members now in the Hall, and they have all expressed deep emotion as they accepted their induction. Tom Kite remembered his boyhood lessons from Harvey Penick, and his long rivalry with Crenshaw, who presented him for induction. Isao Aoki recalled idolizing players like Jack Nicklaus and Lee Trevino, never thinking he might actually compete with them on even terms. Marlene Stewart Streit spoke of how much being the first Canadian inductee meant for her native land.

Charlie Sifford was especially emotional in his induction speech. As a young man, he was denied the chance to play in mainstream professional golf because he was black. He persevered and saw the game's racial barriers lifted.

"You know," he said, "it's a wonderful thing that a little black man from Charlotte, North Carolina, a caddie, can go through all of the obstacles he went through and wind up being inducted into the Hall of Fame. It doesn't get any bigger than that."

The Hall is one of the most powerful ways that golf has devised to transmit its traditions and to show the next generation how high the bar has been set.

SAM SNEAD
is one of the charter members
of the World Golf Hall of Fame,
from the Class of 1974.

"Across the lake, through the trees, we could barely see

Player swing. Then he ran to the edge of the trees to see his shot land on the green. I have never heard a crowd roar like that."

JIM CANSLER,
PGA TOUR FAN
Canton, Georgia

Gary Player (right) often seemed to chase his shots.
Here he watches a tee shot at the 1961 Masters.

Lee Trevino (left), at the 1979 Bob Hope Desert Classic, continued the TOUR's
tradition of star golfers from hardscrabble backgrounds.
Bobby Nichols (above) managed to beat both Arnold Palmer and Jack Nicklaus
in the 1964 PGA Championship. They tied for second.

SAM SNEAD
AND
GARY PLAYER
won more than 100 PGA
TOUR titles between them.

# Fraternity

What was it like on the PGA TOUR in its formative years?

"It was like a fraternity," recalls a player from that era, Bob Toski. "We depended on each other." Toski was a little guy from Northampton, Massachusetts, when he took a shot at touring in the late 1940s, in the era just before television began to transform the game. At the age of 22, he stood 5'6" and weighed 118 pounds after dinner. He recalls going to Florida in his rookie season and joining up with two established players, Ted Kroll and Milon Marusic. Kroll had a Studebaker. They found room for Toski in the backseat.

"I was back there with a clothes rack," he recalls. "I don't know how we got the luggage and the golf clubs into the car. But we did. We shared rooms when we got to the tournament. Kroll and Marusic got the beds. I got a cot."

The players had to split the travel and lodging costs because they had very little money. "We didn't have enough money to count," recalls Toski. "When I asked my wife, Lynn, to marry me in 1953, her mother asked how much money I had in the bank. I said $5,000. Actually, I had $500." A year later, in 1954, Toski was the leading money winner with a little more than $50,000 in earnings. Unlike today, it was less than he could earn as a teaching pro.

But, like many of his contemporaries, Toski remembers the era fondly, thanks to the camaraderie touring fostered. "We had no swing teachers or sports psychologists back then," he recalls. "Ted Kroll was my first mentor. We taught each other out there, and the instruction was simple and to the point. It was about rhythm and tempo. Put the club here, put it there. I remember Ted bragging to Sam Snead about how well he had me hitting it. I learned from the best."

The players of that time took it upon themselves, informally, to enforce certain standards. Toski remembers Lloyd Mangrum, a tough veteran of World War II combat, helping to make sure the golfers looked professional. "If someone would come out in loud clothes, Mangrum might go over to him and say, 'You belong in the circus in that outfit.' We tried to educate the newcomers on how to follow the standards of a professional player."

Those standards were simple and effective like the swing instruction. They remain in effect today. "You were supposed to tip your cap and be conscious of the gallery," Toski remembers. "You had to respect the people who watched. There was no hot-dog stuff, no trash-talking."

They enforced a brisk pace of play. "If Snead or "Jimmie" Demaret were playing with someone who took too much time, they'd sidle over and say, 'On the third waggle, we're walking.'" That was enough to preclude a third waggle.

Bob Toski went on to win the money title in 1954.

**TIGER WOODS**
flashes a smile for his fans. He and
other PGA TOUR players are already
passing on their personal legacies.

ADAM SCOTT

drops to his knees as he watches
a birdie putt slide by the hole at
No. 17 at the 2004 PLAYERS
Championship. He won the title
with a dramatic up-and-down
par on the final hole.

# reaching beyond limits

by

MARK SOLTAU

ERNIE ELS
squints into the gathering
darkness during his playoff with
Tiger Woods at the 2003
Presidents Cup in South Africa

Sunday battles were nothing new for Tiger Woods and Ernie Els. In the 2000 Mercedes Championships, they waged a furious final-day duel, both making eagles at the par-5 18th hole on the windy Plantation Course at Kapalua Resort in Maui, Hawaii. Woods eventually beat Els in sudden death with a long birdie putt.

But at the 2003 Presidents Cup at the Links Course at Fancourt Hotel in South Africa, they took their rivalry a step further. This time they went head-to-head representing their teams, Woods the United States and Els the Internationals. Whoever prevailed in the sudden-death playoff would lead his side to victory after the competition ended in a 17-17 standoff.

Two champions, the clear-cut aces of their respective teams, fighting for pride and bragging rights. And you know what? Neither blinked.

With darkness falling and the tension building, both parred the first two holes. On the third extra hole, Woods showed his greatness by burying a seemingly impossible 15-foot-par putt. Els, feeling the weight of his countrymen on his broad shoulders, matched him from six feet, and the Presidents Cup was declared a tie.

"One of the most nerve-wracking moments I've ever had in golf," said Woods. "Probably the first time I've ever felt my legs shaking a little bit." Els felt it too: "I've never felt more pressure than that. Ever. And I don't want to feel it again."

# Fighting for pride and bragging rights.

Ernie Els and Tiger Woods line up putts during the 2003 Presidents Cup, an event that forced both of them to test their limits in team play.

Most PGA TOUR players are adept at handling the heat, and in many cases raise their games to a higher level. Whether it's Tiger Woods hitting a 6-iron out of the bunker over water at the 2000 Bell Canadian Open, Shaun Micheel flagging a 7-iron to within inches of the cup on the 72nd hole of the 2003 PGA Championship, or Aussie Craig Parry slam-dunking his second shot into the hole at the par-4 18th to edge Scott Verplank in a playoff at the 2004 Ford Championship at Doral, golfers have a way of rising to the occasion, and often they do it in spectacular fashion.

How do they do it?

"I guess it's just if you do it on a bigger stage, like the last hole, it gets extra fanfare because a lot of people play this game and know how hard it is," says Verplank. "To do stuff like that is definitely out of the ordinary. And to be able to do something out of the ordinary on that kind of stage makes it that much more remarkable."

Many factors contribute to the heroic shots, including fitness instructors, nutritionists, swing coaches, sports psychologists, and technological advances in equipment. Today's professional is better prepared, mentally and physically, to perform at a higher level.

"I think it happens in all sports," says 2003 U.S. Open champion Jim Furyk. "Maybe it's more dramatic in golf because everyone has to be quiet. Whether you're hitting a buzzer-beater in basketball or riding the moment as a football team, it happens in all sports. It's confidence, probably. The people that do it all believe they can."

Craig Parry's par putt on the 15th hole during the 2004 Ford Championship at Doral kept him close, and he won by holing out from the 18th fairway in a playoff.

A lot of people play this game and know how hard it is.

SHAUN MICHEEL
raises his 7-iron triumphantly on
the final hole of his win at the
2003 PGA Championship.

In the 1999 Ryder Cup match between the United States and Europe, Justin Leonard made his clutch forty-five-foot birdie putt on the 17th hole at The Country Club near Boston to clinch the American win. Leonard dug deep and delivered the knockout punch because he had heart, talent, and a never-say-die attitude.

"You draw on the fact that you've done it Tuesday through Saturday, you've done it a million times with your buddies," Jeff Sluman says.

Even with a great support group, golfers are independent contractors who have no teammates to lean on. They earn every penny and stand alone in pressure situations. In the final round of the 1982 U.S. Open at Pebble Beach Golf Links, Tom Watson chipped in on the 17th hole for a birdie to hold off Jack Nicklaus. Was it luck? Not if you ask Watson, who'd practiced similar chips thousands of times.

"At that point you're more focused and you're only into one thing, and you're looking at the pin," says Sluman, winner of the 1988 PGA Championship. "Especially if you're in a situation where you have to do it or you're probably not going to win the golf tournament. Those are situations where heroic things happen."

# Heart, talent, and a never-say-die attitude

Tom Watson, renowned for finding ways to get the ball out of trouble and into the hole, blasts from a bunker at the 1994 AT&T Pebble Beach National Pro-Am.

"The ultimate role model

is being yourself.
Be honest with yourself
and others."

D A V I D   D U V A L

Former world number one David Duval gauges a putt.
His PGA TOUR record includes 13 victories.

Gio Valiante, a professor of psychology at Rollins College in Florida, works with a half-dozen PGA TOUR pros, including Leonard, Chris DiMarco, Chad Campbell, and Charles Howell III. He believes advances in sports psychology have been pivotal in helping players achieve maximum success.

"It's unquestionable," Valiante says. "When properly applied, no question it can take golfers and get them to play at a higher level. Have I helped every golfer? No. But I've helped 90 percent."

Valiante helps his clients deal with anxiety, fear, and stress. If not addressed, all can lead to problems with grip pressure, the ability to make a full swing, and releasing the club. "When arousal gets too high, you see a physiological change in people," he says.

In the past, most sports psychologists concentrated on declarative knowledge, essentially telling clients what they needed to do to improve. Now, they have shifted to procedural knowledge, explaining how to improve. "It's not enough to tell someone they need to be confident," says Valiante.

Fran Pirozzolo has worked for the New York Yankees and more than a handful of golfers, including Bernhard Langer, Mark O'Meara, and Hank Kuehne, on the mental side of sports. He has another theory about maximizing potential and performing under pressure.

"It starts with the idea of focusing on the physical, not the mental," Pirozzolo says. "It gives a lot of guys hope that you don't have to fight the demons."

Pirozzolo also helps them simplify their lives. "We always try to get a handle on the outside stuff and put a label on it so they don't have that feeling of being overwhelmed," he says. "You're not going to be very focused if you have a lot of unfinished business."

# It's not enough to tell someone they need to be confident.

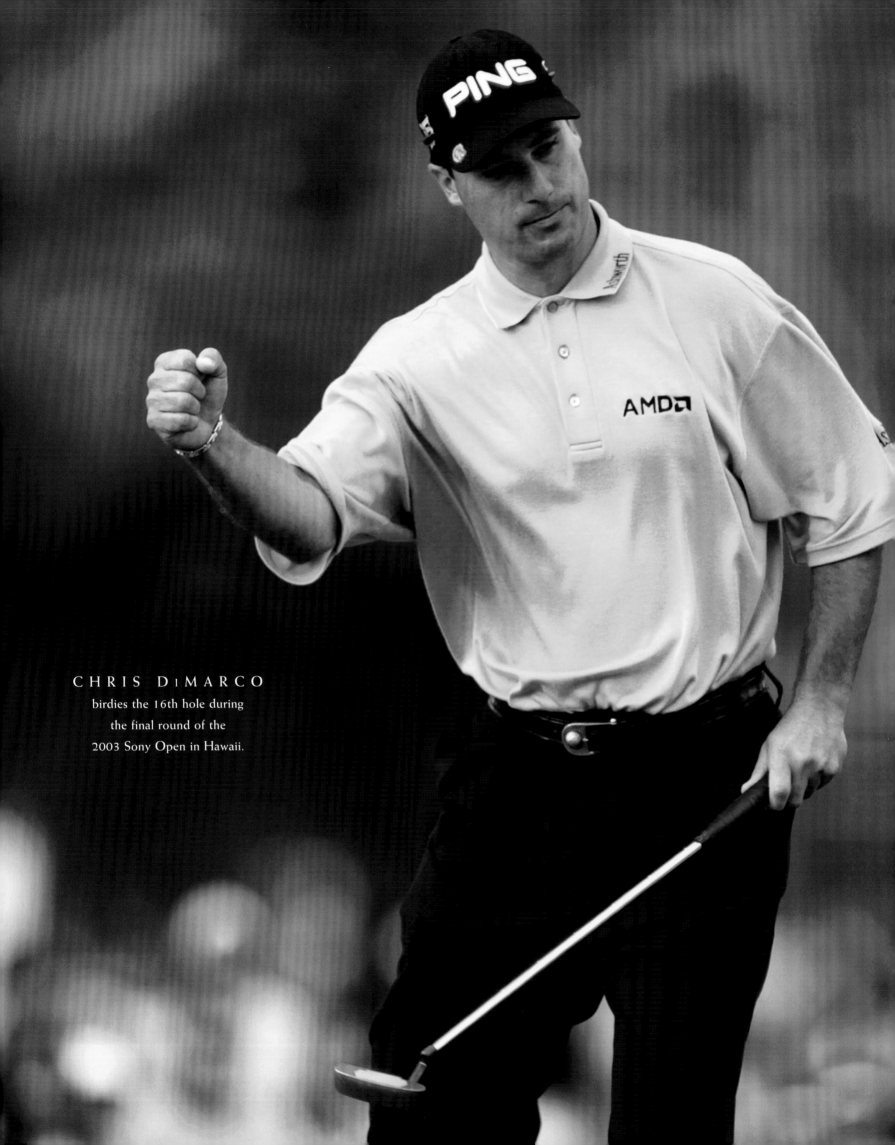

CHRIS DiMARCO
birdies the 16th hole during
the final round of the
2003 Sony Open in Hawaii.

AARON BADDELEY
made his debut on the PGA TOUR at
the age of 18 and shot a pair of 62s
at the 2003 Valero Texas Open.

Advances in equipment have made golf slightly easier at the highest level, consequently making it that much more difficult for the best golfers to separate themselves from the pack.

"I think people are getting more out of their games for a lot of different reasons," says Laird Small, director of the Pebble Beach Golf Academy and the 2003 PGA National Teacher of the Year. "Fields are deeper; someone will shoot a good score no matter what. The ball has changed, allowing players to go directly at the flag. Plus, they are hitting 8-irons 170 yards. I think you're going to see a lot more 59s and 58s in competition."

Small also predicts more younger players will start working with sports psychologists in high school and college. Combine that with better equipment and a good work ethic, and it seems only natural scores will go down.

"As the kids are becoming involved and engrossed, there's going to be casualties along the way," Small says. "They get burned out or stuck. It's a lot of hard work to get it fixed. But that's part of the pursuit of greatness."

One of Small's teaching mantras is NATO, which stands for "not attached to the out-come." Too often, golfers psyche themselves out by getting too wrapped up in a shot or score instead of playing each shot as it comes and enjoying the ride. "I think that's a huge thing for people's performance from a spiritual and performance side," he says.

## Too often, golfers psyche themselves out.

Nick Price came to the PGA TOUR from Zimbabwe and had one of golf's great seasons in 1994, winning six times, including the British and Canadian Opens and the PGA Championship.

Due to equipment regulations, few players have an extra edge. "It's coming down to the skill of the player because equipment is becoming more even across the board," Small says. "If someone wants to get better, they have to work harder."

Those who make the PGA TOUR have paid a price. Once they are there, the sky is the limit.

"It seems to me that every time we watch a major on television, the announcers say, 'That's the most heroic shot of all time,'" says Howell. "And the next major, they say the same thing.

"It's the drama and the setup. Sometimes you'll see shots as good as that hit Sunday morning at 10 A.M. by the first group out, but there's not the drama, there's not the fanfare. There's not any of the attention. It's hitting a great shot under the right circumstances. It's hitting the shot under pressure."

If someone wants to get better, they have to work harder.

Jim Furyk celebrates as his bunker shot drops at the 2001 World Golf Championships-NEC Invitational.

**SERGIO GARCIA** wins the 2001 Buick Classic with a three-stroke lead. He went on to become the youngest player to win $2 million in a season.

# The full circle

Adam Spenner is surrounded by souvenirs of the TOUR, given to him by the players he has inspired.

David Duval was all smiles. He has struggled gamely through injuries that have cost him the form and focus that made him the world's number one golfer a few years ago. This time he was in a match not just of drives, chip shots, and putts, but a showcase of courage and perseverance that epitomizes the game. The PGA TOUR had arranged a special charity match for television that partnered Duval with Special Olympian Kevin Erickson against Duval's father, Champions Tour player Bob Duval, who was teamed with Special Olympian Oliver Doherty.

Duval had sliced his first tee shot of the day into the rough, but his partner bailed him out with a drive to the middle of the fairway. "Fairways are overrated," Duval quipped.

Erickson, who won the U.S. Golf National Invitational in Florida, is a twenty-one-year-old who was born with a tumor and had a third of his brain—the area that affects speech and motor control—removed as an infant. Then when he was eighteen he was diagnosed with cancer in his sinuses. He played golf throughout his treatments and has grown into a 12-handicap golfer.

Doherty was born with brain damage and partial paralysis on his left side after his mother was killed in a car accident before he was born. His adoptive father, Jim Doherty, gave Oliver a golf ball to squeeze when he was a child to develop strength. Soon he was holding a club, and now he's a 5-handicap golfer and the 2003 Special Olympics World Summer Games champion.

David Duval and Erickson won the match when Erickson holed a birdie putt on the 16th hole. The match was, Duval said, his best round of golf in 2004, and the best trophy of all was perspective. "I've always felt I was a strong guy," Duval said. "But I'm not as strong as these two men."

Another inspiring source of perspective for PGA TOUR players is Adam Spenner. At age 21, "15th Tee Adam," victim of a brain stem tumor, has outlived his life expectancy by 18 years. He can't play golf—he can't even hold a club—but there is no more avid PGA TOUR fan. Adam, a quadriplegic, surfs the web by navigating with his chin to check the field, tee times, and scores of each PGA TOUR tournament. TOUR players at tournaments in Wisconsin all know that Adam will be waiting at the 15th tee, and they often stop to sign memorabilia for his burgeoning collection. At Whistling Straits, Jerry Kelly jumped the gate to sneak up behind Adam's wheelchair and put his arms around him. As Bret Quigley told Adam's mother, Linda, that day, "You don't know how much Adam means to us."

So the inspiration comes full circle, and those who give are those who get.

**DAVID DUVAL**

gave Kevin Erickson his caddie bib on which he
had written, "Kevin, thanks for including me
in a great day." Erickson gave Duval perspective.

CHARLES HOWELL III
reacts to the tension at the
World Golf Championships.

# Breaking sixty

Al Geiberger admires the plaque at Colonial Country Club that commemorates his round of 59.

"Not a day goes by that I don't talk about it," Al Geiberger says.

It happened on June 10, 1977, in sweltering heat during the second round of the Danny Thomas Memphis Classic at the demanding Colonial Country Club in Cordova, Tennessee. He made eleven birdies and one eagle on the 7,282-yard par-72 course and went on to win the tournament. During one stretch, he posted a then-PGA TOUR record of six birdies and an eagle. From then on, Geiberger became known as "Mr. 59," and he still hands out business cards with a little scorecard on them.

Geiberger played near-flawless golf that summer day. He hit every fairway and green in regulation, using only 23 putts. Normally, he uses at least three golf balls per round. That day, he used one. "I was rolling so good, I didn't want to change," he says.

And while the lift, clean, and place rule was in effect that day, allowing players to improve their lie in their own fairway, Geiberger didn't take advantage of it. "I was in a place where I never thought I would hit a bad shot," he says. "I felt invincible."

In the middle of his round he was eight under for seven holes, and suddenly his gallery began to swell. Even some of his fellow competitors came out to watch.

He recalls, "From the 14th green to the 15th tee, I remember having a little talk with myself. I said, 'What have you done?' I just decided to pull out all the stops and let it go, see what I could shoot. I just became aggressive, which is not my nature. When I birdied 15, the gallery started yelling '59!' That was the first time it entered my mind."

With temperatures hovering above 100 degrees and the humidity stifling, Geiberger kept plugging along. While he felt drained, the fans gave him energy. It was so hot, Geiberger remembers a nearby grass field catching fire and a half dozen cars burning during that week.

A former PGA Championship winner, Geiberger came to his final hole, the par-4 ninth, needing a birdie to shoot 59. After splitting the fairway off the tee, he knocked his second shot ten feet from the cup and faced a tricky left-to-right putt into the grainy bermudagrass. Playing partners Dave Stockton and Jerry McGee watched breathlessly as Geiberger stroked the ball into the center of the hole.

"That putt was so easy to leave short," Geiberger, who still plays on the Champions Tour, says. "I remember telling myself, 'Don't leave it short.'"

AL GEIBERGER
tees off during the 1976 Masters
the year before he recorded his
record low score.

Two images of Ernie Els (left) watch the action at the 2004 Sony Open.
Nick Price (above) vents his frustration on his putter at the
2004 Nissan Open in Los Angeles.

JOHN DALY

displays his power as he hits from a
bunker in 2004.

# Connecting two worlds

The J. Erik Jonsson Community School helps nurture the future of North Oak Cliff.

There are more than a handful of buildings located in the North Oak Cliff neighborhood just south of downtown Dallas that carry the ugly scars of inner-city graffiti. Yet there's a building at 106 East 10th Street that remains untouched. It's not because the building is a small target. At 74,000-square-feet, it takes up almost an entire block. It's because what happens every day inside the building has earned the respect of the entire community. It's success is almost entirely due to one of the strongest relationships ever developed between a charity and a PGA TOUR event.

The building at 106 East 10th Street houses the J. Erik Jonsson Community School, one of the community service projects of the Salesmanship Club of Dallas. All of the net proceeds from the EDS Byron Nelson Championship—and in 2004 that totaled just over $6 million—benefit the Salesmanship Club Youth and Family Centers (SCYFC), a non-profit organization founded in 1920. The centers provide education and mental health services for children and their families in the greater Dallas area.

The Jonsson Community School is the centerpiece of this effort. It's an accredited, research-based laboratory school serving approximately 260 children, from three-year-olds through sixth grade students. It also hosts two family therapy clinics, one in the same building as the school, and another in northwest Dallas, where licensed therapists provide counseling for children and family members with a wide range of mental health needs.

It all costs money. The money provided by the Salesmanship Club of Dallas makes up more than 92 percent of SCYFC's $8.5 million operating budget. "We wouldn't exist without those funds. We would be a fifth of our size without it. It is our bread and butter," said Dr. Kent Skipper, executive director of the SCYFC. "It also ensures that no child is turned away because of financial considerations."

The EDS Byron Nelson Championship provides more charity money than any other tournament on the PGA TOUR, and the Salesmanship Club has been awarded the Benefactor Award by the PGA TOUR Tournaments Association four times.

While fifteen miles may separate the lush fairways of the Tournament Players Club Four Seasons Las Colinas and that highly regarded, graffiti-free building on East 10th Street, the connection between the two vastly different worlds could not be closer.

**BYRON NELSON**
wears his hat from the
Salesmanship Club of Dallas when
he presides over the EDS Byron
Nelson Championship each spring.

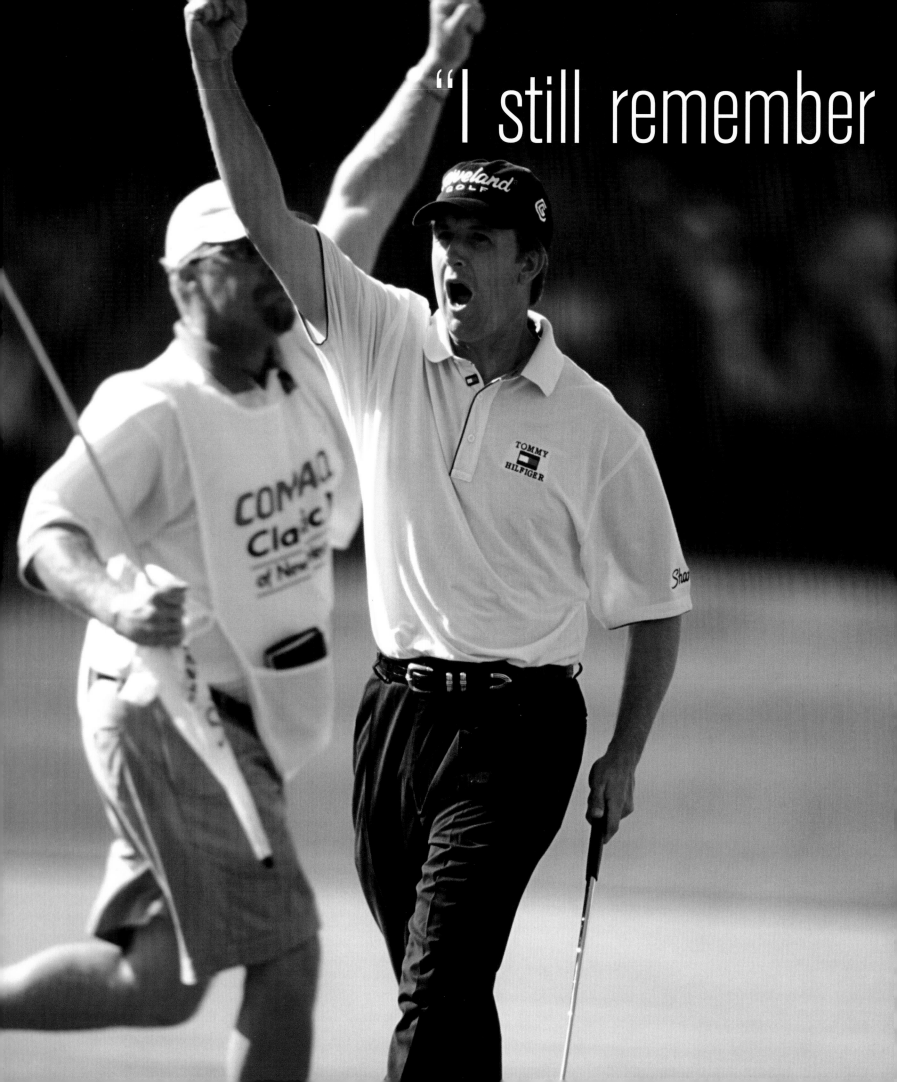

"I still remember

Toms putting his hand
in the air.
I knew I was seeing
something special."

BRYAN MITCHELL,
PGA TOUR FAN
Slidell, Louisiana

David Toms and caddie Scott Gneiser celebrate victory at the
2001 Compaq Classic in New Orleans.

# The dream

Chip Beck lines up a putt during the Nissan Los Angeles Open at the Riviera Country Club in 1994.

**Chip Beck had a childhood dream:** shooting 59. Beck grew up and followed another dream—that of becoming a professional golfer. He joined the PGA TOUR in 1979 and in the spring of 1991, during his thirteenth year on the TOUR, his wife, Karen, had a premonition about her husband shooting 59. It all became reality on October 11, 1991, in the third round of the Las Vegas Invitational. Beck made thirteen birdies and no bogeys at the 6,914-yard par-72 Sunrise Golf Club and wound up tied for third.

The thirty-five-year-old Beck started on the back nine and shot a 7-under-par 29. After opening birdie-par, he reeled off six straight birdies and then parred No. 18. On the front nine, he went birdie-birdie-par-birdie, made two pars, then birdied the last three holes. "It was extraordinary, to be honest with you," he says. "The further I get away from it, the more extraordinary it gets."

Having competed for the victorious U.S. Ryder Cup two weeks earlier, Beck came to Las Vegas in great spirits. During a practice round, he and fellow competitor John Cook talked about how it might be possible to shoot 59 at Sunrise, but neither believed it would happen. They also discussed a million-dollar bonus put up by Hilton Hotels Corporation for any player breaking 60.

On the par-4 10th hole, Beck's first of the round, he made a sixty-foot birdie putt, and he knew something special was possible. "That was the big key," he said. "It was like the floodgates opened up."

After his sparkling front nine, Beck didn't know what to expect. "Twenty-nine is the kiss of death," he says. "I was real nervous."

He kept the round going with a fifteen-foot par putt at No. 15, then made a tough, big-breaking 10-foot birdie putt at the par-3 17th. When he reached No. 18, he knew what he had to do.

Following a good drive, Beck figured he had to hole out his second shot because the greens were getting spiked up due to the pro-am. He nearly did, but was left with a tricky, three-foot downhill putt. Sensing the enormity of the moment, his pro-am partners picked up so Beck wouldn't have to wait. And, sure enough, there were two spike marks in his line.

"The only thing I said to myself was, 'Just give this a chance,'" he recalls. "I just stayed steady on it. Seeing the spike marks actually made me focus better." Beck credits his caddie, Dave Woosley, for guiding him around the course and keeping him calm. "He knew how to manage the course and my game," says Beck, who gave Woosley the ball afterward. "I followed his direction and didn't get ahead of myself."

Even happier about getting back into contention in the tournament than shooting 59, Beck celebrated by going to a practice area to hit balls. Word of his score had spread quickly, and the guys running the range were surprised to see him.

"You can't charge this guy for balls," said one. "He just shot 59."

"I was just really happy that night," Beck says. "I slept really well. That memory will last a lifetime."

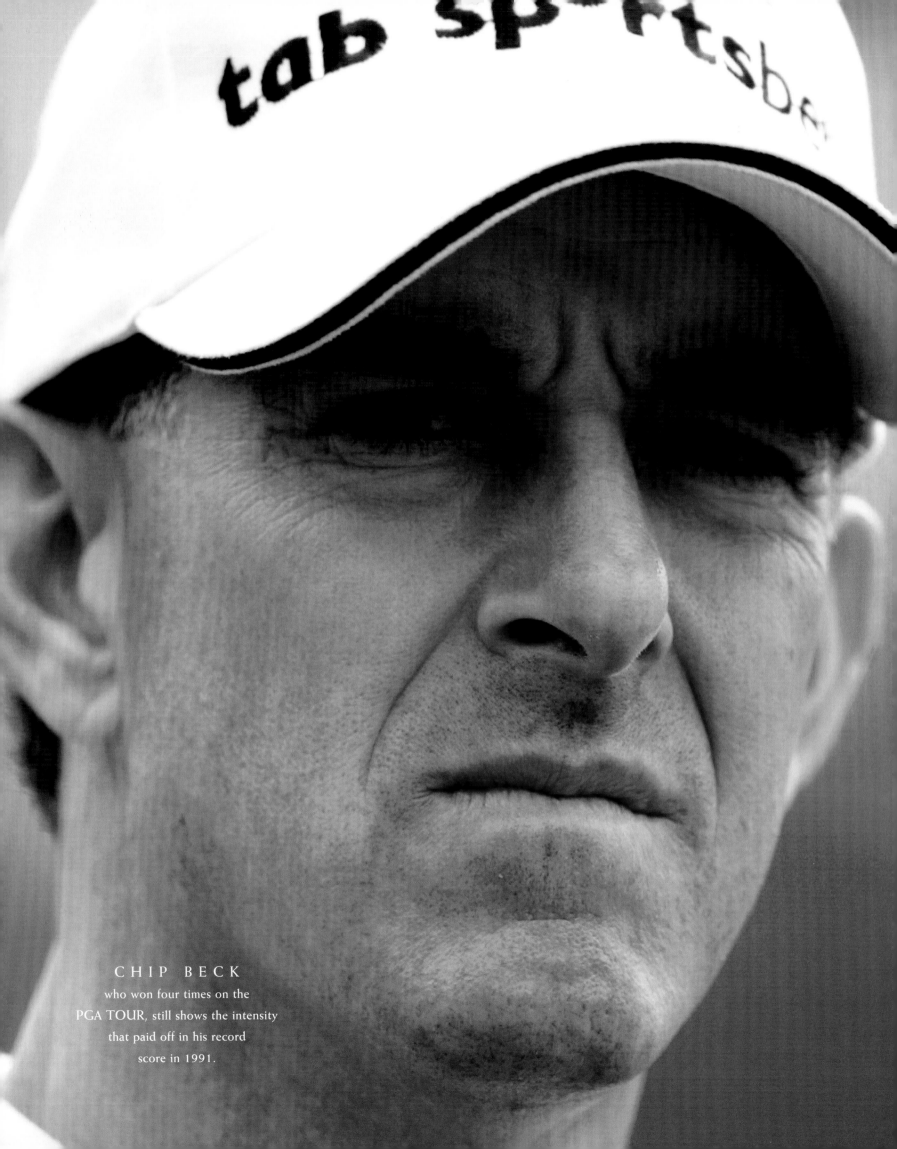

CHIP BECK
who won four times on the
PGA TOUR, still shows the intensity
that paid off in his record
score in 1991.

# More than just a score

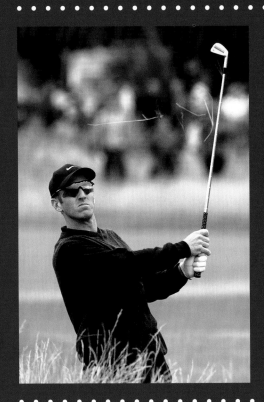

David Duval is an extremely accurate iron player when he's on, as he showed by winning the 2001 British Open.

It was a cool January day in 1999 at the Bob Hope Chrysler Classic at the Palmer Course at PGA West in La Quinta, California. David Duval looked equally cool, as usual, but behind his wraparound sunglasses he was "a little juiced" as he walked down the fairway of the par-5 18th hole. Then, as he floated his 5-iron near the pin, the crowd along the fairway and green erupted. The ball sat eight feet from history, and the spectators went quiet as Duval stepped up.

He didn't hesitate. The putt split the hole and dropped for an eagle, and the usually reserved Duval pumped his fist, then raised both arms in celebration. He had matched Al Geiberger and Chip Beck for the lowest round in PGA TOUR history and in the process he had overcome a seven-stroke final-round deficit to win by one stroke.

Shooting a 59 had never entered Duval's mind, and certainly not that day. "I got out to the driving range having played the first four rounds in 13 under [the tournament is 90 holes] and not having played all that well, and I wasn't hitting it all that great on the range, so I just tried to loosen up."

During the opening round, Duval had been plagued by putting problems, but that all changed on the first hole on Sunday. He recalls, "I hit it up there about five feet and had a little downhill, left-to-righter and thought, 'Man, you need to start making a couple of these.' And after that, I just kept going." The longest putt Duval made all day was a 12-footer for birdie at No. 14.

"I don't know if I was in the zone, but I was certainly dialed in," Duval says. "Every shot I hit was next to the hole. It wasn't like I was making putts. It was two feet, eight feet, three feet, two feet, one foot. Everything was real close."

Duval was relaxed from start to finish, and everything seemed to fall into place. "The yardages were fairly spot-on most of the day," he says. "The lines were straight because the putts were short. That's kind of how it was."

Low rounds were nothing new for Duval. In the 1997 AT&T Pebble Beach National Pro-Am, he fashioned a 10-under-par 62 in the third round at Pebble Beach Golf Links to tie the course record.

As time goes on, Duval feels greater appreciation for what he accomplished. Just don't expect him to raise the subject in conversation.

"It's just a round of golf," he says. "It's neat that I did it; not very many people have. I have the ball, glove, and scorecard in a little shadow box in my house. It's more than just a score, obviously."

**DAVID DUVAL**

sinks an eagle putt on the final hole
to win the 1999 Bob Hope Chrysler
Classic with a final-round 59.

A sand bunker isn't the only place where a player employs the explosion shot. Shigeki Maruyama blasts from the water (left) at the World Golf Championships-World Cup in 2001. Retief Goosen (above) plays the more traditional shot at THE TOUR Championship of 2004, which he won.

TOMMY ARMOUR III

watches a putt during the
2001 Nissan Open.

# A week to remember

**Tommy Armour III never saw it coming.** Not after missing six of eight cuts in the U.S. Open, withdrawing from a seventh tournament after an opening-round 79, and tying for 36th in the other.

True, the grizzled forty-three-year-old Texas resident tied for 11th at the Reno-Tahoe Open two weeks before the 2003 Valero Texas Open and had begun to trust a swing change orchestrated by instructor Mike Abbott, the general manager at the Vaquero Golf Club in Dallas. Abbott had told Armour he was taking the club back too far inside, resulting in pull-hooks.

Once he started trusting the change, Armour felt more comfortable with his swing. Still, he entered the Texas Open ranked 157th on the PGA TOUR money list, and he seemed more intent on making the cut than the record books.

As it turned out, he made both. Playing at La Cantera Golf Club in San Antonio, a hilly, par-70 course, Armour opened with a 64, three strokes behind Bob Tway and Heath Slocum, who equaled the course record with 61s. The next day Armour shot a 62 to secure a one-stroke lead, and he wasn't done. He followed with a 63, matching the PGA TOUR 54-hole record-low total at 189, and bolted to a six-shot advantage.

Although temperatures cooled off to the low 80s on Sunday, Armour stayed hot. He kept firing at the flags and carved out a closing-round 65, good for a seven-stroke win over Loren Roberts and Tway. Armour's 26-under-par total of 254 bettered PGA TOUR's 72-hole scoring mark of 256 set by Mark Calcavecchia at the 2001 Phoenix Open. He also shattered the tournament scoring record by three shots.

"It just kind of happened," Armour said. "I can't explain it. I just stayed with one shot at a time the whole tournament, you know, the old cliché, but that's basically what it was. I just stayed in the moment and hit a lot of good golf shots."

Armour credits Fran Pirozzolo, player development coach for the NFL's Houston Texans, for helping with his concentration. "He helped me empty my mind and just play each shot as it comes," he says.

Armour didn't make a bogey the first three rounds. He finally made one Sunday, three-putting from 45 feet on the par-4 10th hole. Admittedly, Armour didn't miss many putts. For most of the week, the hole seemed as big as a manhole cover.

"I never really got ahead of myself," says Armour. "I just kind of plodded along. I don't really fluctuate emotionally on the course, so it wasn't anything new for me."

Afterward, it was a different story. Armour took over a Dallas restaurant and celebrated with friends into the early-morning hours.

Not the sentimental type, Armour didn't keep any mementos of the tournament other than his putter and the trophy. "It was just one of those weeks," he says. "I wish I could push that button a lot more."

Tommy Armour III was still smiling months after his record score when he competed at the 2004 Mercedes Championship, an event for tournament winners only.

VIJAY SINGH
was the Player of the Year in 2004,
breaking the $10 million barrier in season
earnings and winning nine tournaments,
including the PGA Championship.

4: Robert Beck/Sports Illustrated
7: Donald Miralle/Getty Images
8: Jim Gund/Sports Illustrated
10: Robert Beck/Sports Illustrated
12: © Kevin LaMarque/Reuters/Corbis
16: Bob Martin/Sports Illustrated
20: Getty Images
22: © Kevin LaMarque/Reuters/Corbis
24: John W. McDonough/Sports Illustrated
25: Copyright Unknown/Courtesy USGA. All rights reserved.
26: Getty Images
27: Getty Images
28: © Bettmann/Corbis
29: Hy Peskin/Time-Life Pictures/Getty Images
31: Stuart Franklin/Getty Images
32: © Bettmann/Corbis
33: © Bettmann/Corbis
35: PGA TOUR Images
36: Al Tielemans/Sports Illustrated
37: Jim Gund/Sports Illustrated
39: Chuck Solomon/Sports Illustrated
40: Getty Images
41: Getty Images
43: Stuart Franklin/Getty Images
44: Ronald Martinez/Getty Images
45: Getty Images
46:: Darren Carroll Photography
48: Getty Images
49: Scott Halleran/Getty Images
50: © Bettmann/Corbis
52: Chris Stanford/Allsport/Getty Images
55: © Chris Trotman/Corbis
56: PGA TOUR Images
57: Getty Images
58: Getty Images
59: Getty Images
60: David Cannon/Allsport/Getty Images
61: Getty Images
62: Robert Beck/Sports Illustrated
64: Darren Carroll Photography
66: Darren Carroll Photography
67: Getty Images

68: Getty Images
69: Harry How/Getty Images
70: Roberto Schmidt/AFP/Getty Images
72: Getty Images
73: Simon Bruty/Sports Illustrated
74: Getty Images
75: Getty Images
76: Darrin Braybrook/Allsport/Getty Images
78: Getty Images
79: Malcolm Clarke/Keystone/Getty Images
80:: Andrew Redington/Getty Images
82: Getty Images
83: Getty Images
85: Donald Miralle/Getty Images
86: John Biever/Sports Illustrated
87: Jim Gund/Sports Illustrated
88: PGA TOUR Images
89: Getty Images
90: Bob Martin/Sports Illustrated
92: Jim Bourg/Getty Images
93: Getty Images
95: Harry How/Getty Images
96: © Walter Iooss for StocklandMartel.com
97: Getty Images
98: Andrew Levine Photography
99: Andrew Levine Photography
100: AP/Wide World Photo
102: PGA TOUR Images
104: Getty Images
106: Getty Images
107: Harry How/Allsport/Getty Images
108: Stonehouse Publishing
110: Edward M. Pio Roda/Getty Images
111: © Gary Newkirk/NewSport/Corbis
112: Getty Images
113: Russell Kirk Photography
114: Getty Images
115: Getty Images
116: Bob Martin/Sports Illustrated
117: Donald Miralle/Getty Images
118: Photograph copyright Joann Dost
120: Jerry Morgan

121: Getty Images
122: Photo by Evan Schiller
123: Darren Carroll Photography
124: Getty Images
125: Getty Images
126: Scott Halleran/Getty Images
129: John Biever/Sports Illustrated
130: Stuart Franklin/Getty Images
131: Getty Images
132: www.HawkinsProductions.com
134: Brian Bahr/Getty Images
136: Getty Images
137: Jeff Gross/Getty Images
138: Bob Martin/Sports Illustrated
139: Robert Beck/Sports Illustrated
140: Getty Images
141: Stephen Dunn/Getty Images
142: J. D. Cuban/Sports Illustrated
144: Bob Gomel/Time-Life Pictures/Getty Images
146: Scott Halleran/Getty Images
147: HistoricGolf.com
148: Getty Images
149: Scott Halleran/Getty Images
150: Getty Images
152: Bob Martin/Sports Illustrated
154: Getty Images
155: A. Y. Owen/Time-Life Pictures/Getty Images
156: James Drake/Sports Illustrated
157: Getty Images
159: Gabriel Benzur/Time-Life Pictures/Getty Images
160: E.P. Schroeder/Pix Inc./Time-Life Pictures/Getty Images
161: Streeter Lecka/Getty Images
163: © Bettmann/Corbis
164: Harry How/Getty Images
165: Getty Images
166: Walter Iooss Jr./Sports Illustrated
167: HistoricGolf.com
168: © Walter Iooss for StocklandMartel.com
170: © Phil Cannon
171: © Bettmann/Corbis
172: Jeff Gross/Getty Images
174: © Walter Iooss for StocklandMartel.com

175: © Walter Iooss for StocklandMartel.com
176: Art Rickerby/Time-Life Pictures/Getty Images
177: HistoricGolf.com
178: Darren Carroll Photography
180: Malcolm Clarke/Keystone/Getty Images
182: Stuart Franklin/Getty Images
183: Getty Images
184: Getty Images
185: Scott Halleran/Getty Images
186: Getty Images
187: Getty Images
188: David Cannon/Allsport/Getty Images
191: Getty Images
192: Adam Pretty/Allsport/Getty images
193: Getty Images
194: © Reuters/Corbis
195: PGA TOUR Images
196: Courtesy Adam Spenner
197: © Sam Greenwood Photography
198: J. D. Cuban/Sports Illustrated
200: Photograph courtesy of Phil Cannon,
     Tournament Director, FedEx St. Jude Classic
201: HistoricGolf.com
202: Donald Miralle/Getty Images
203: Robert Beck Photography
204: Tim Sloan/AFP/Getty Images
206: © Gracie Reyna
207: Gary Bogdon/Sports Illustrated
208: PGA TOUR Images
210: Getty Images
211: Mark Dadswell/Getty Images
212: Jamie Squire/Getty Images
214: Getty Images
215: Harry How /Allsport/Getty Images
216: Bob Martin/Sports Illustrated
217: © Tami Chappell/Reuters/Corbis
218: Jeff Gross/Getty Images
219: PGA TOUR Images
220: Darren Carroll/Sports Illustrated
224: Harry How/Allsport/Getty Images